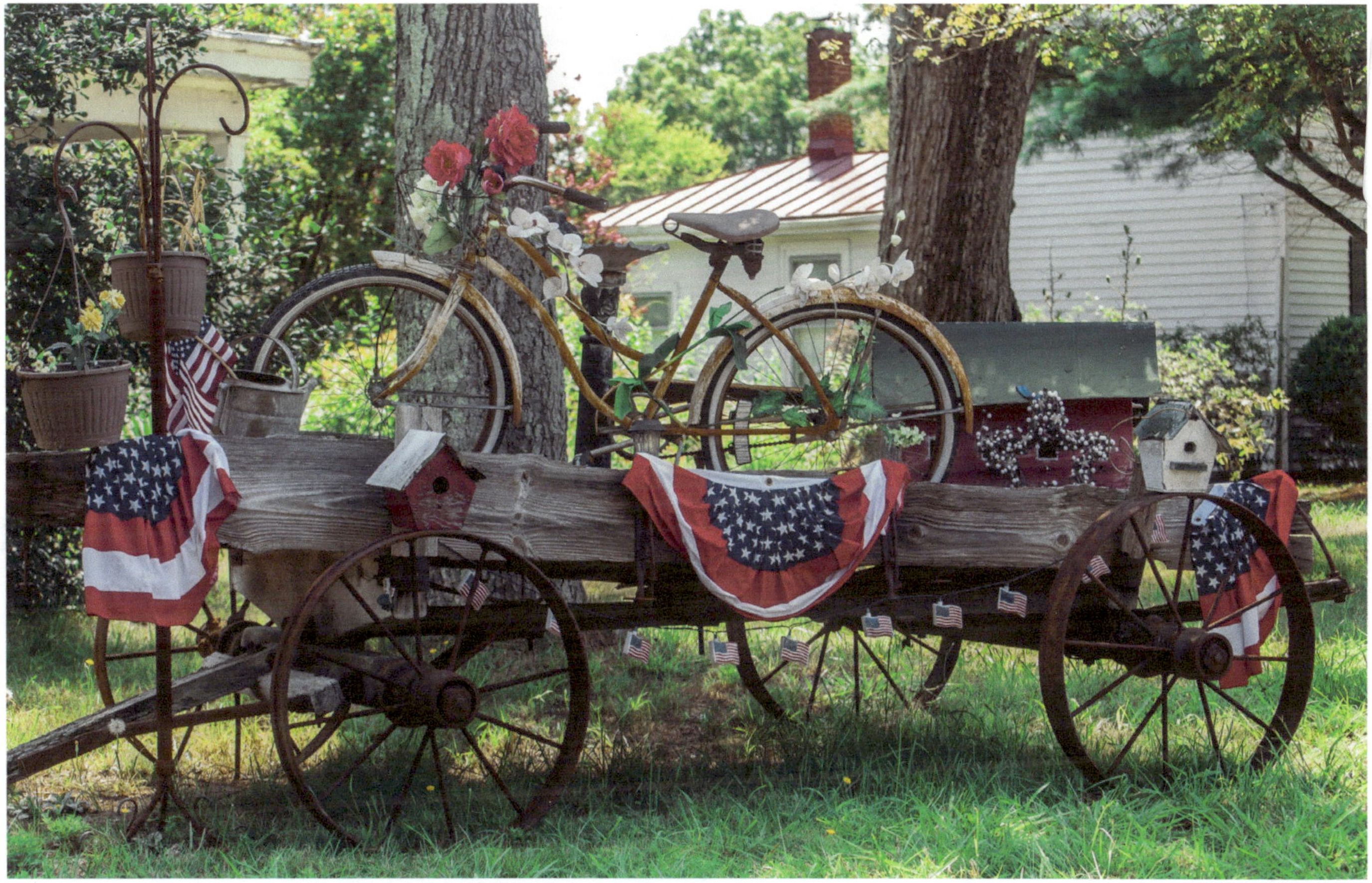

Journeying Home via Alternate Routes

Shirley Nan Washington, Ed.D.

Copyright Page

Copyright 2021 by Shirley Nan Washington

All rights reserved. This book or any portion thereof may not be reproduced or used in any manner whatsoever without the express written permission of the author or publisher.

Preface and Acknowledgments

PREFACE:

Can you remember the last time you took a different route home from work or play? Do you choose traveling the interstate highways versus the state highways? Do you ever wish to view more beautiful scenery as you travel the roads and the world?

While traveling home from the Washington DC metropolitan area to Harrisonburg, Virginia, the author had consistently taken I-495 (Capital Beltway) to I-66 (west) to I-81 (south) for more than 20 years. It was in August 2015 when she concluded she recognized several of the landscapes from that same itinerary and wanted to explore another route home.

Her journey also changed because of the horrendous traffic. She changed her course of direction from I-495 to U.S. Route 50 (west) instead of I-66. The adventure was less crowded and more picturesque. After reaching Middleburg, she continued her scenic drive, wandering the twists and turns through Virginia's byways.

This photographic book was created to showcase and share the beautiful countryside views, historical sites, specialty eateries, etc. that she discovered from taking alternate routes from Silver Spring, Maryland to her home in Harrisonburg, Virginia.

ACKNOWLEDGMENTS:

The author wishes to express her appreciation to her Extended Essay instructors, Brian V. Jones and Harry St. Ours of Montgomery College, for their direction, supervision, and encouragement with the production and editing of this photographic book. In particular, her gratitude also goes to Charles Harried and his assistants at the Takoma Park-Silver Spring Academic Computer Lab for their technological assistance; and to her sisters Bernice, Mary Ann and Jean, for their support and continuing reinforcement.

About the Author

The author, Shirley Nan Washington, '78 Ed.D. (UMASS), is a native of Harrisonburg, Virginia and resides in Silver Spring, Maryland. She is a retired educator and lifelong learner who is a six-time Montgomery College graduate (with honors) from the following programs of study: Paralegal Studies ('12); Criminal Justice ('13); Photography ('15); Studio Art ('18) General Art ('19) and Communication Studies ('20). Dr. Washington is a recipient of several awards, including: the Dr. Harry Harden Jr. Academic Excellence Student Medallion (2013), the Spirit of Service Medallion for Student Volunteer Service Hours (2016), and Studio Arts Award for Demonstrating Outstanding Academic Performance in the Studio Arts (2019).

Since her undergraduate studies at Virginia State University, Shirley has been actively involved in community affairs and social justice. She holds a Charter Membership in the Smithsonian's National Museum of African American History and Culture and has membership in other organizations, including: ACLU, MSEA and NEA. Her national honor society memberships include Lambda Epsilon Chi (LEX), Phi Delta Kappa, and Phi Theta Kappa. She served 13 years as Ombudsman Representative (volunteer) with the Montgomery County Long Term Care Ombudsman Program (Maryland Enhanced Certification), and she is also a former member of the Wheaton Library Advisory Committee (8 years).

Besides having a great appreciation for the visual arts: capturing photographic images of distinctive sights and sounds, creating works of art, visiting museums, etc., Shirley also enjoys playing the piano, mingling with diverse folks, and learning about drones. She has had photographic and art pieces showcased in juried student exhibitions and in the Sligo Journal.

Shirley reminisces her childhood's love of travel and fascinating art through her vividly dazzling photography. Her three colorful, photographic books showcase road trips' images from some of Virginia's finest and rarest antiques, magnificent arts, unique animals, and scenic views of the Shenandoah Valley and nearby regions. In her 184-page photographic book trilogy, Home, she revisits some of the same Virginia towns she toured as a youngster and shares findings of her picturesque journey.

Introduction

This photographic book contains 39 images of antiquated objects which were immediately appealing, eye-catching, to the author on her driving tour of some of Virginia's U.S. highways, backstreets, and alleys within the Shenandoah Valley and Piedmont regions of Virginia. The images are identified, to the best of her knowledge, on each page and are presented in the following sequence:

Historical Churches, pp. 1-4
Heavily Textured Structures, pp. 5-8
Antiquated Vehicles, pp. 9-13
Unusual Structures, pp. 14-19
Decorative Front Porches, pp. 20-23
Community Centers pp. 24-25
Old Time General Stores, pp. 26-29
Printing Presses, pp. 30-31
Unique Signs, pp. 32-33
Specialty Eateries, pp. 34-37
"Home, Sweet Home," p. 38-39

As you journey with the author while viewing her photographs, she hopes you will also find joy and beauty in the ancient automobiles, structures and objects of the like that are often found on backstreets.

She invites you to consider exiting the major interstates for the U. S. highways in order to explore more unique sights, smells and sounds.

vi

HISTORICAL CHURCHES

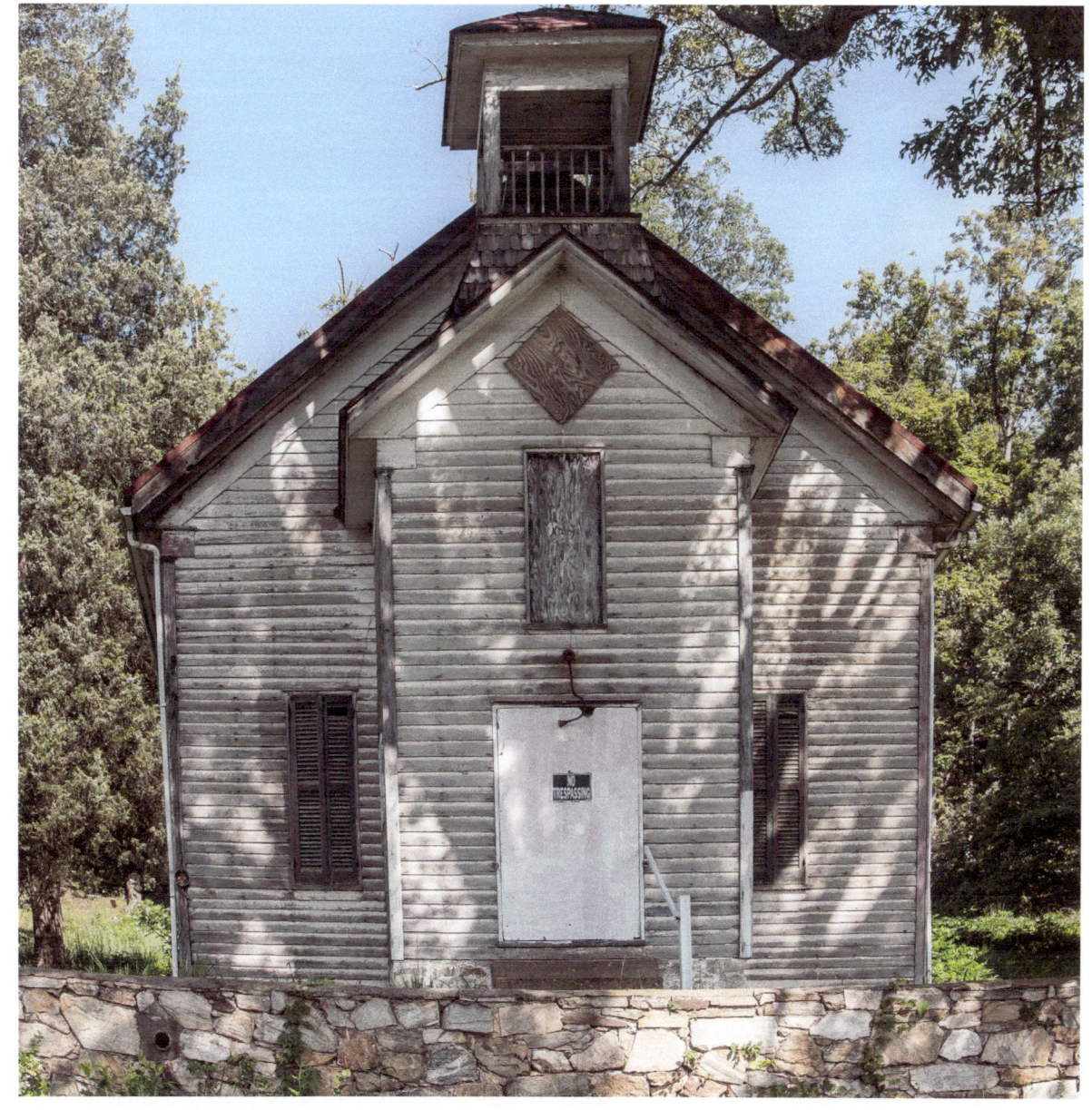

Mt. Pleasant Baptist Church, ca. 1875, Bowmantown, VA

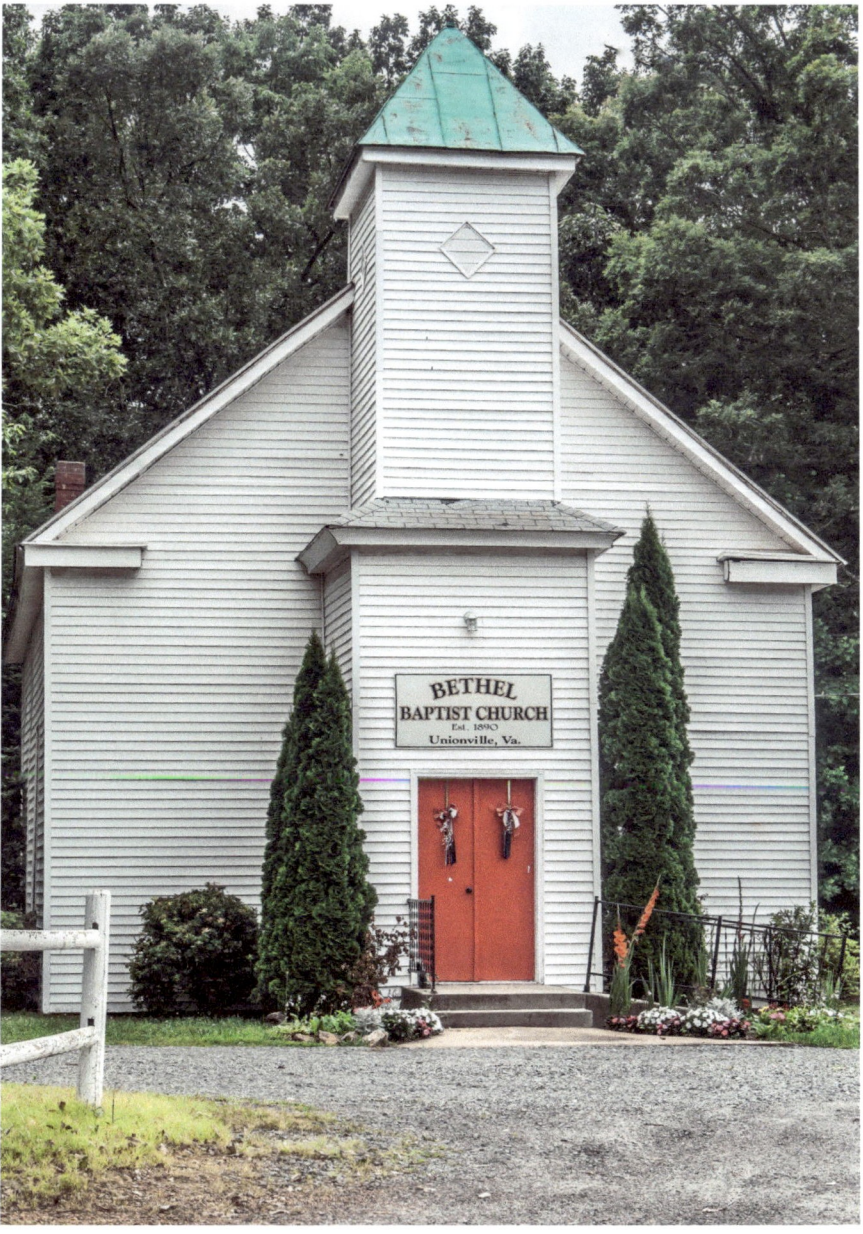

Bethel Baptist Church, ca. 1890, Unionville, VA

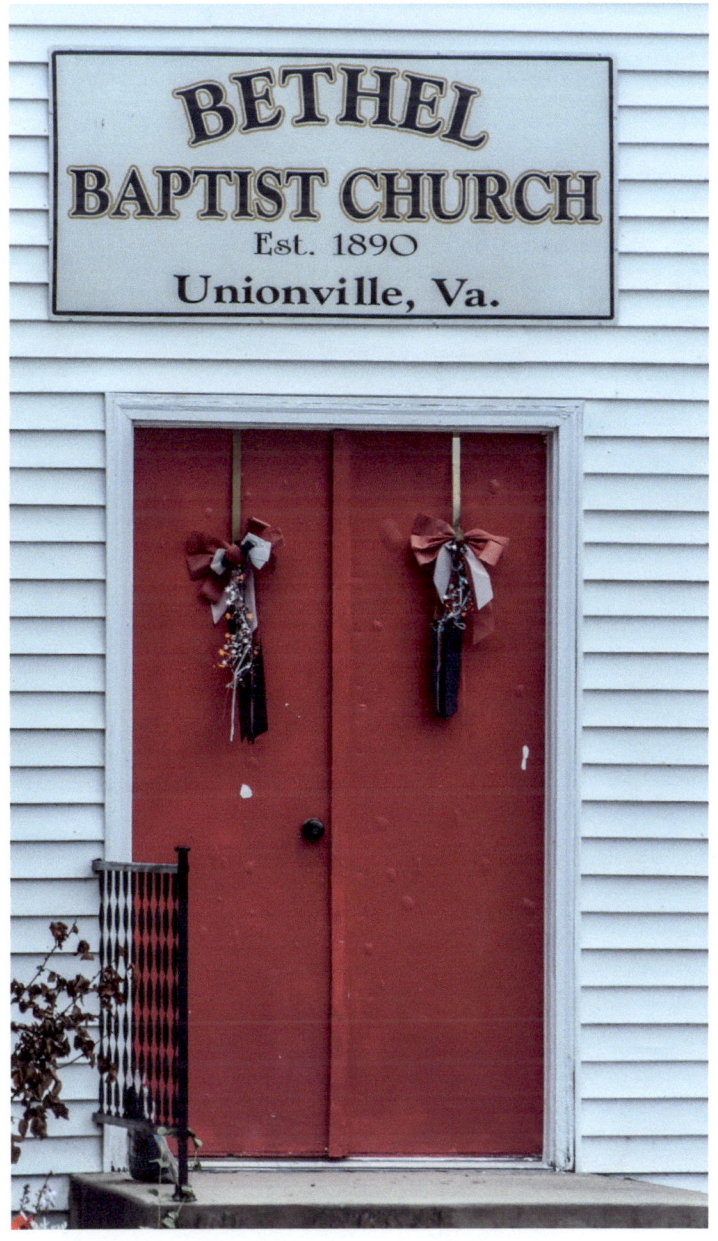

Bethel Baptist Church's Front Door

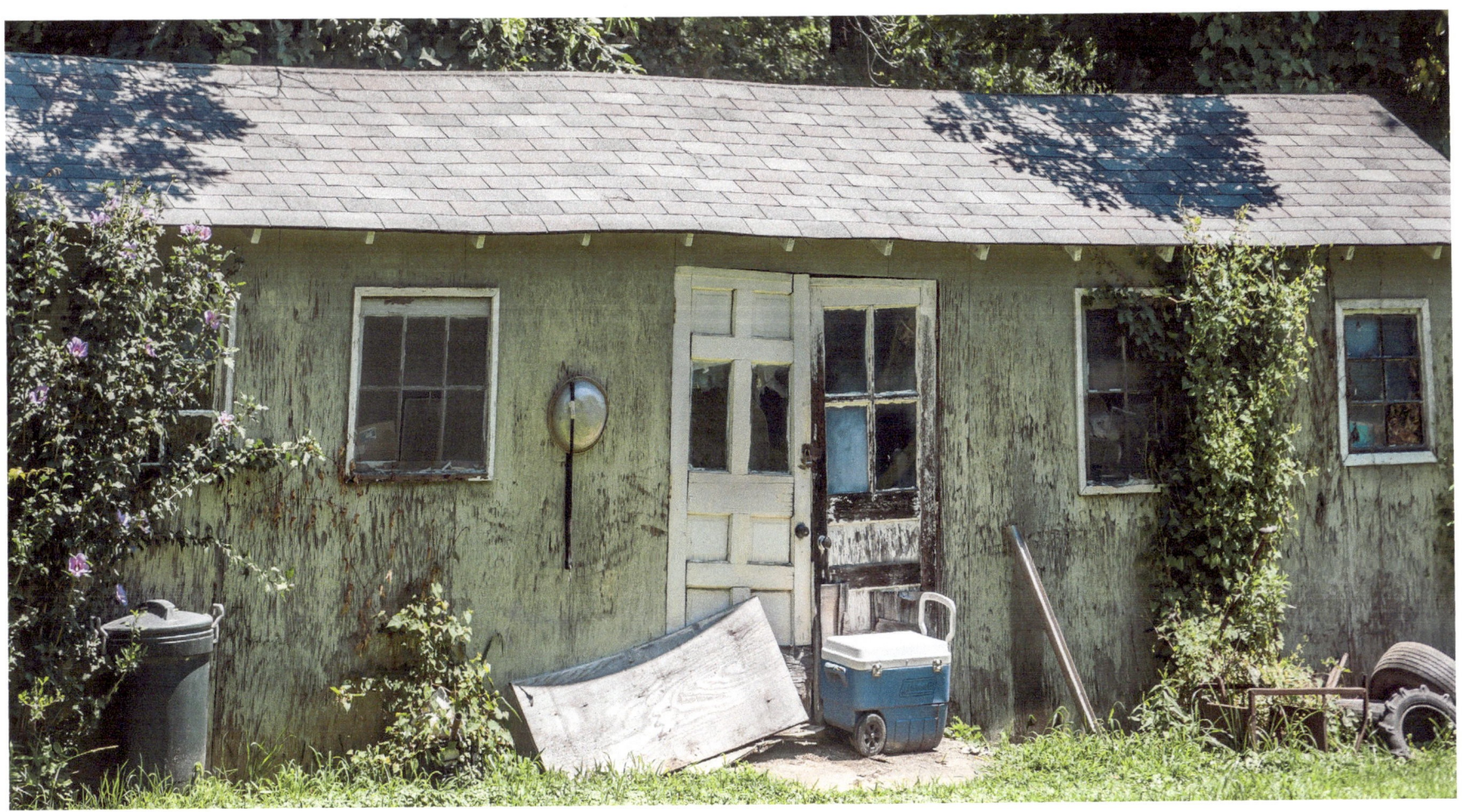

"Green Door Church," Macsville, VA

HEAVILY TEXTURED STRUCTURES

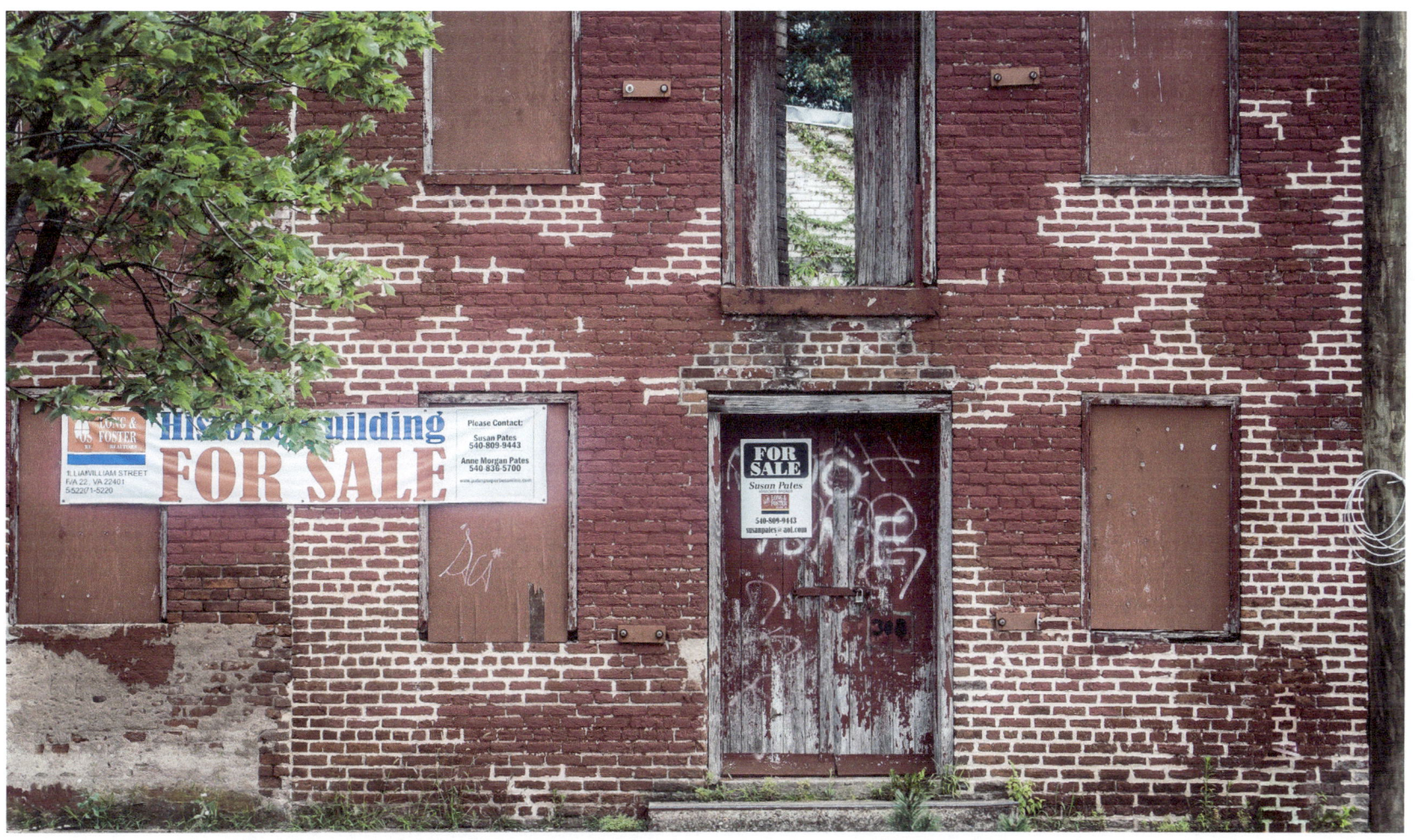

Historic Building For Sale, Fredericksburg, VA

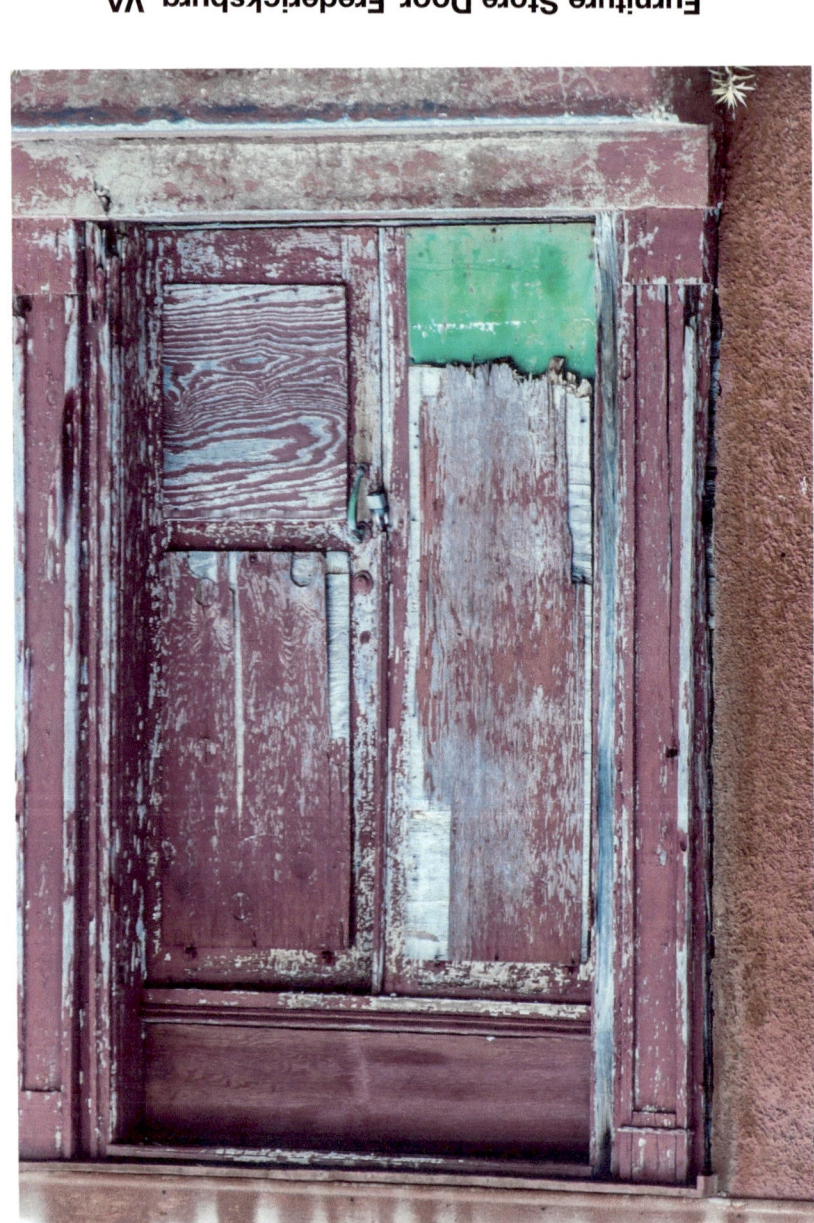

Furniture Store Door, Fredericksburg, VA

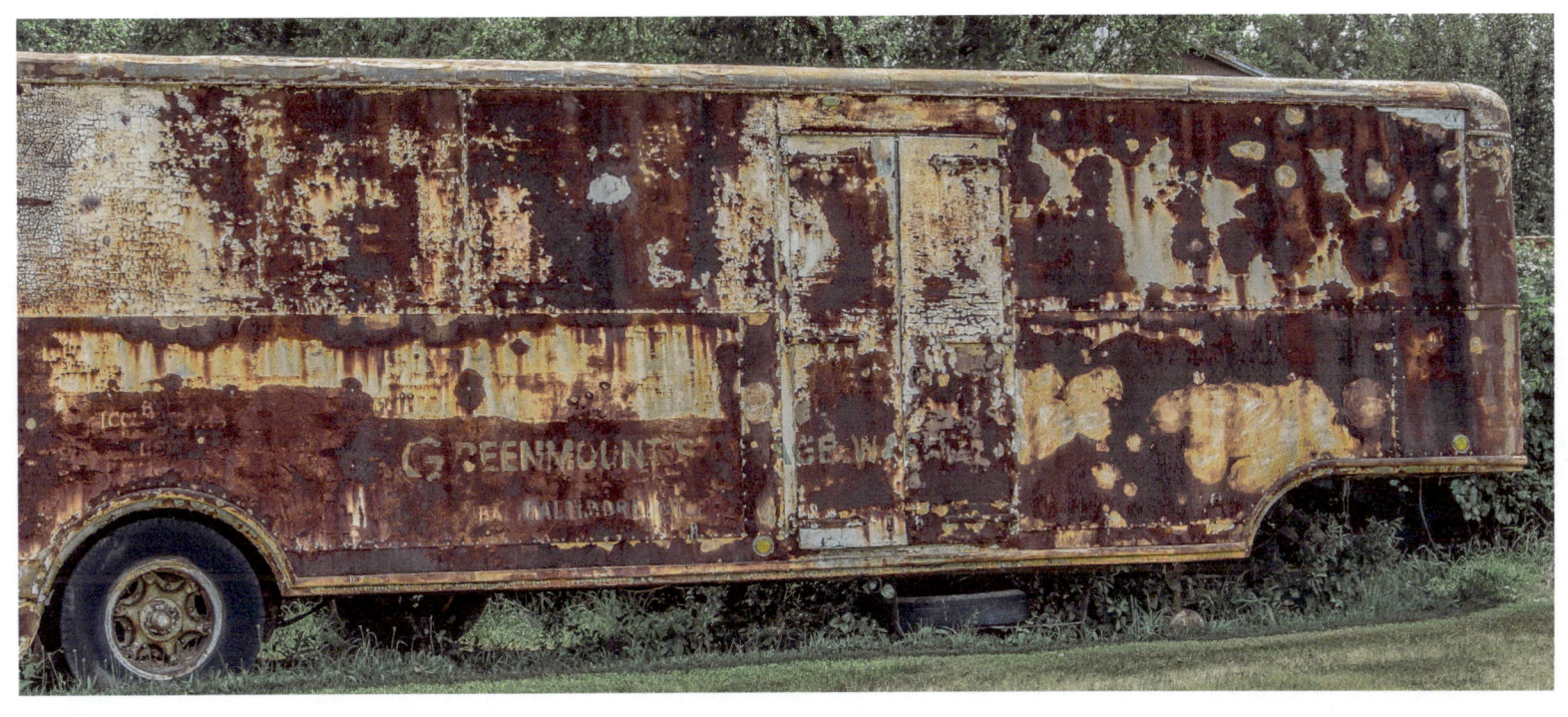

Mural Bus, Milford, VA

Vintage Chairs, Millwood, VA

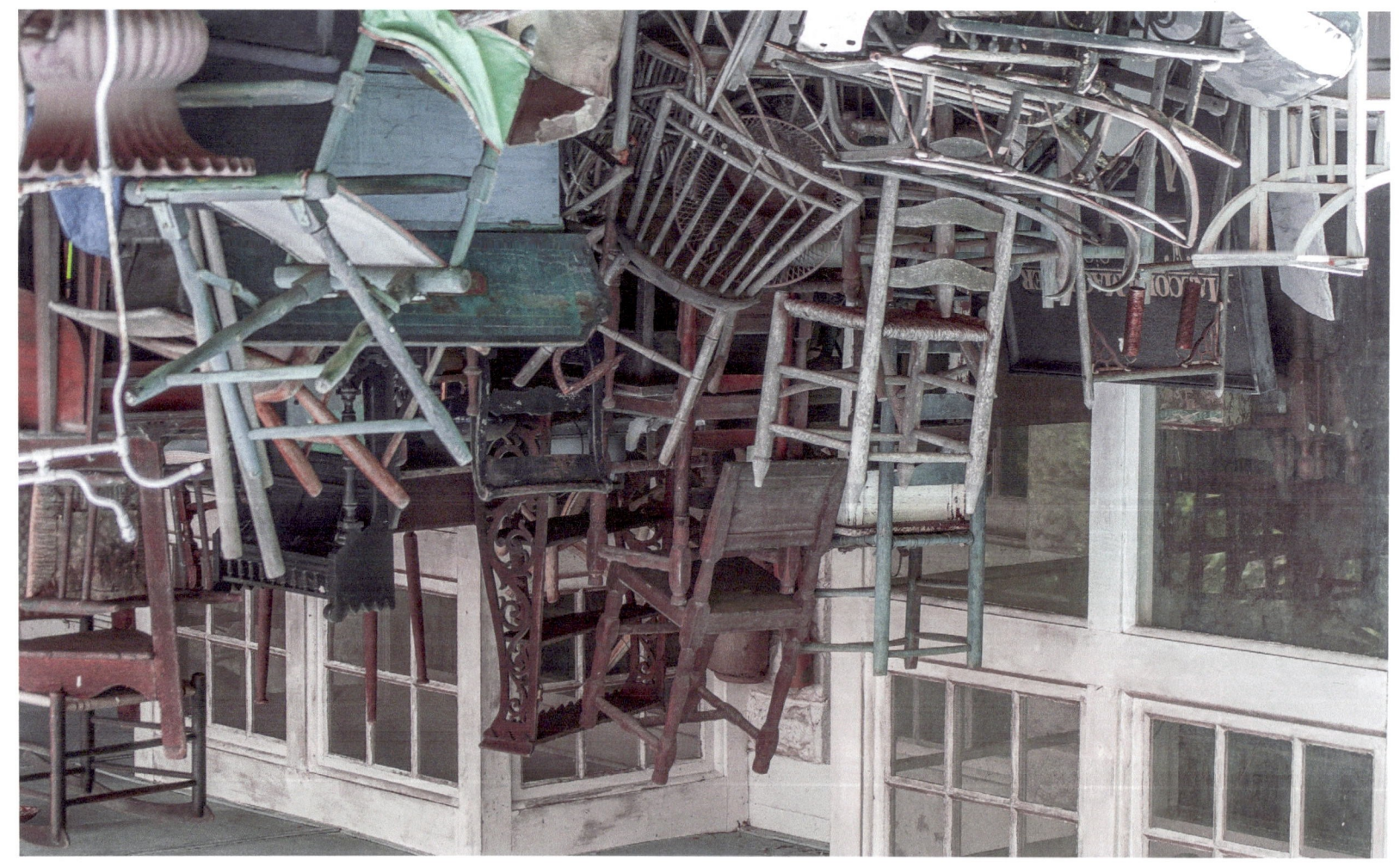

ANTIQUATED VEHICLES

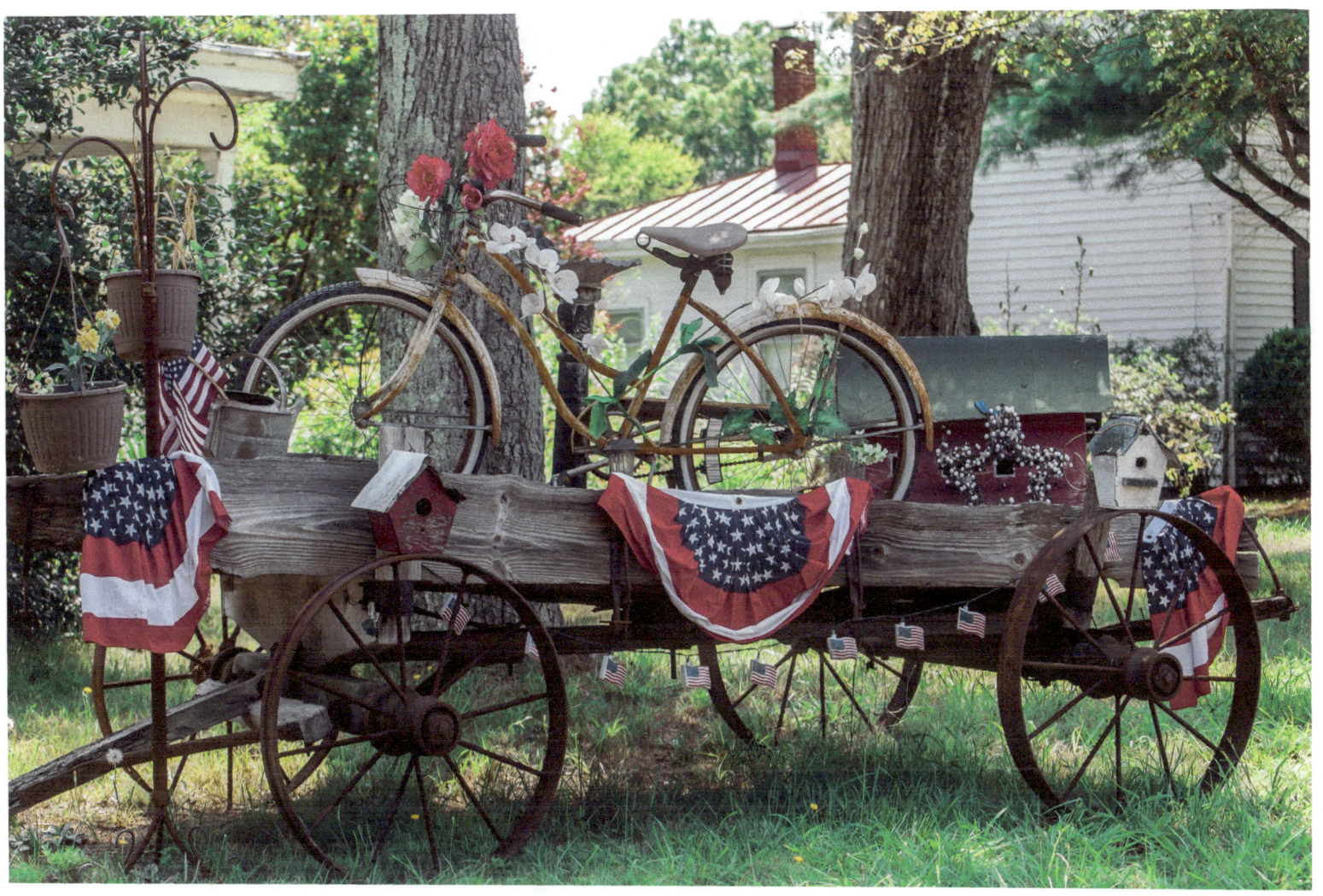

Antique Wagon Wheels and Vintage Bike, Caroline County, VA

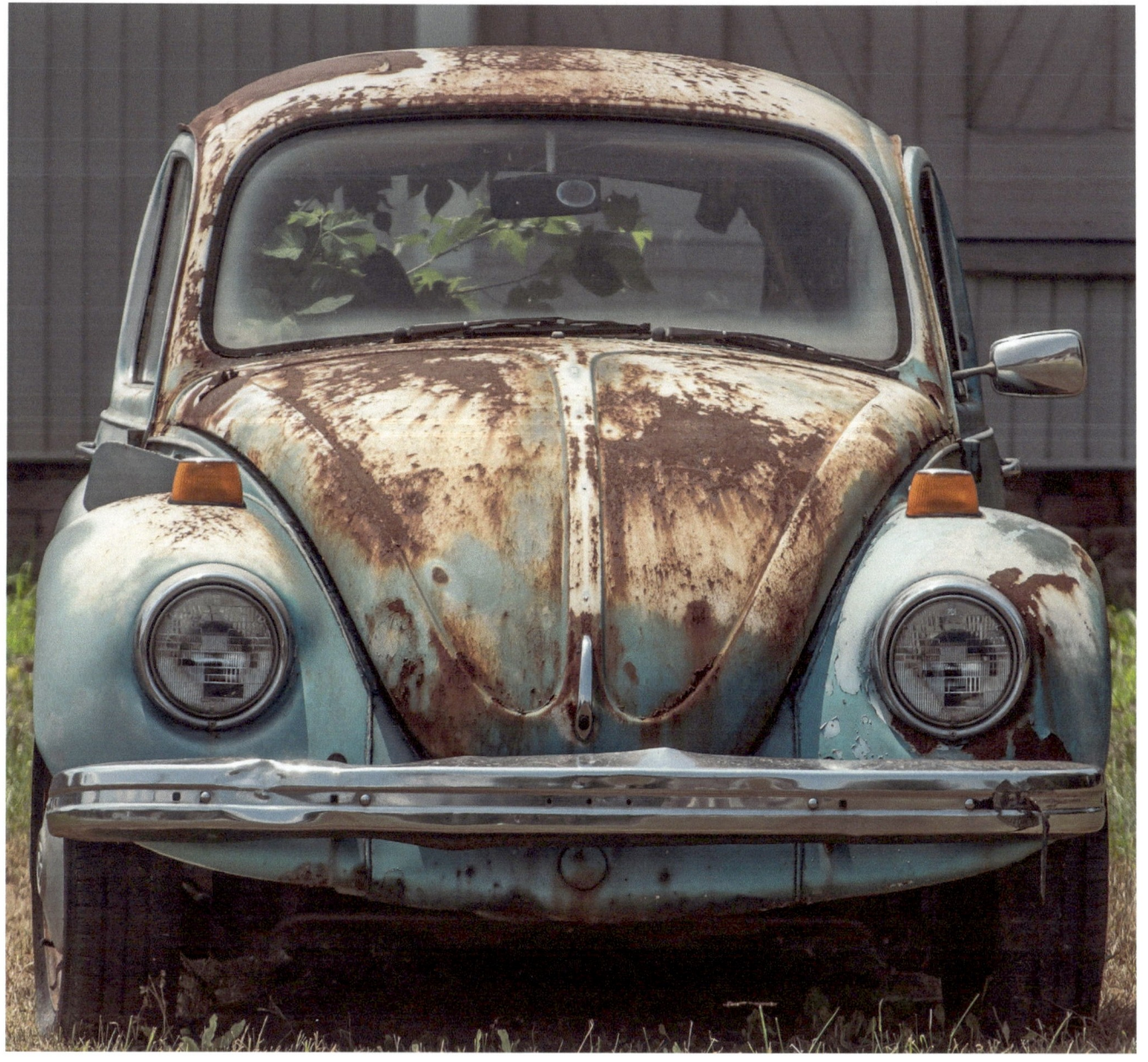

Rusty VW Beetle, Milford, VA

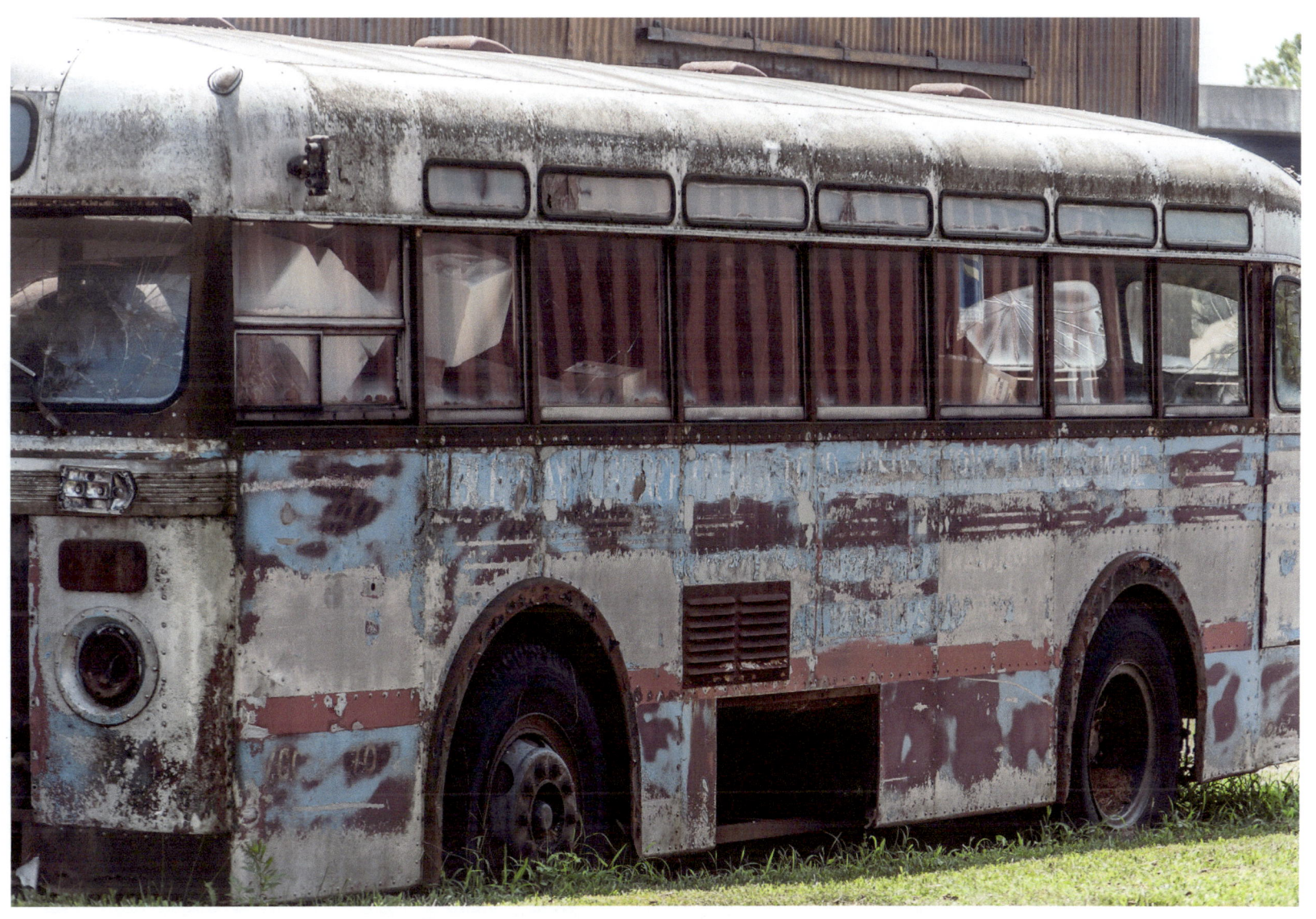

Vintage Trailer Bus, Milford, VA

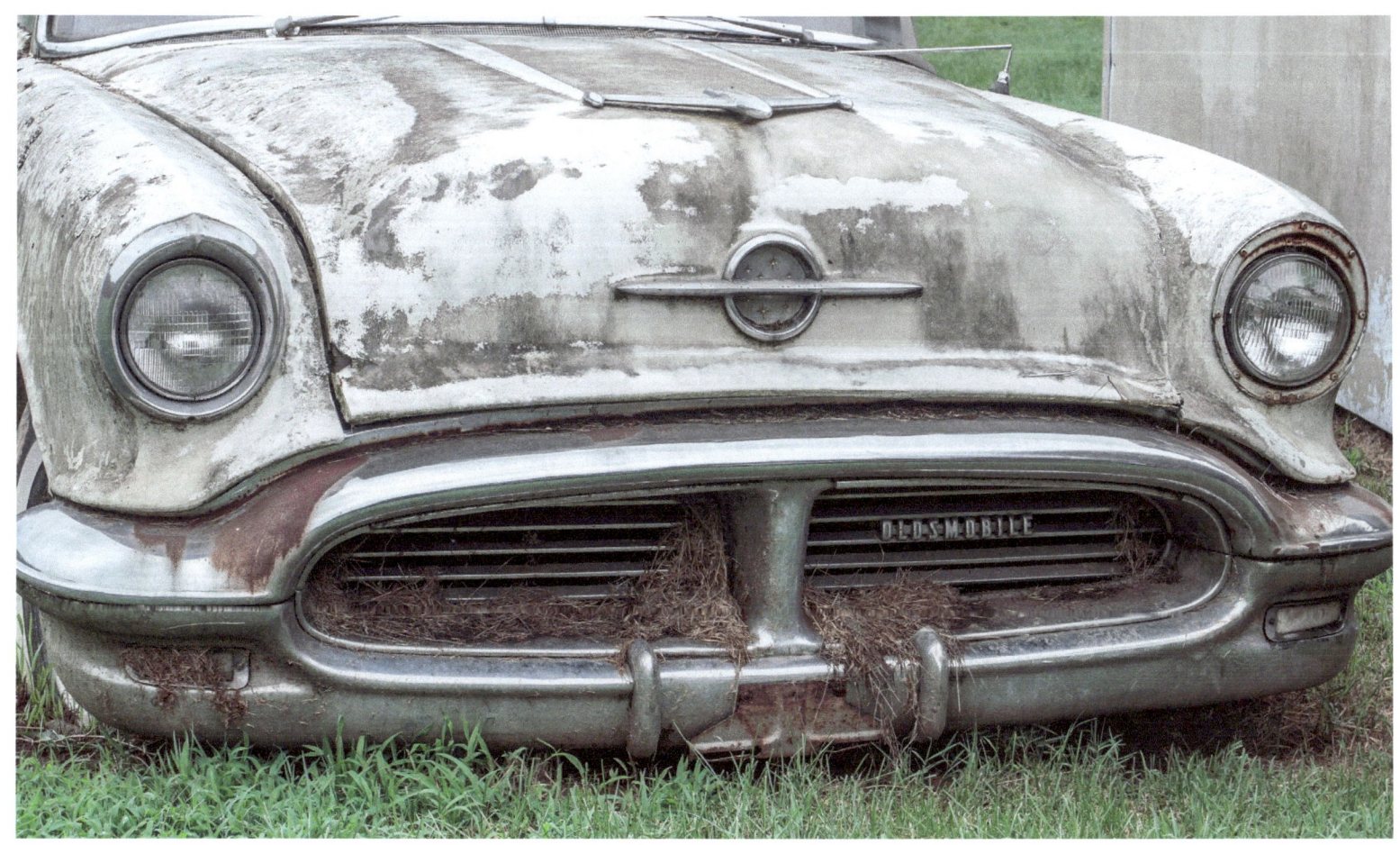

1956 Oldsmobile, Spotsylvania, VA

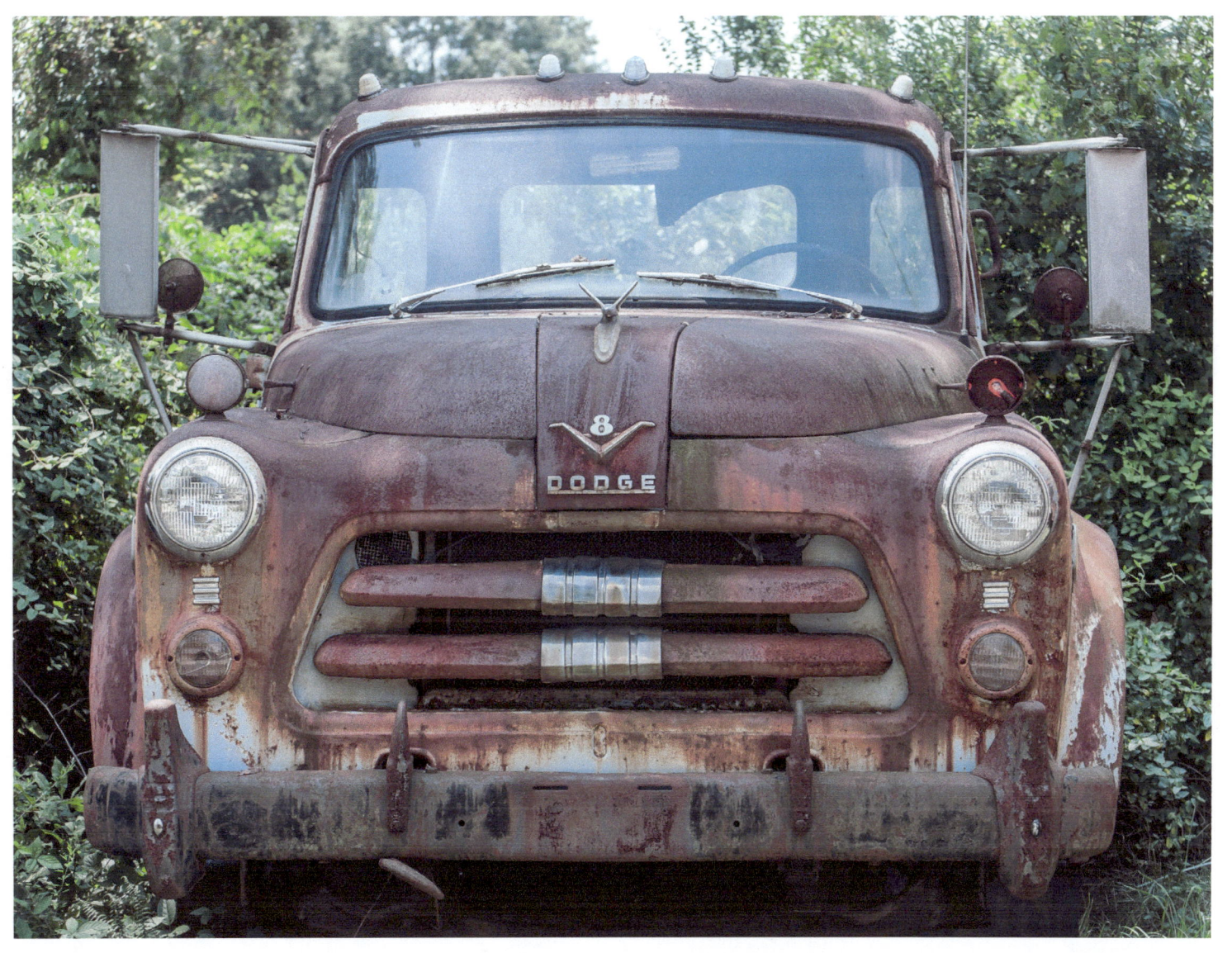

1956 Dodge Pickup, Milford, VA

UNUSUAL STRUCTURES

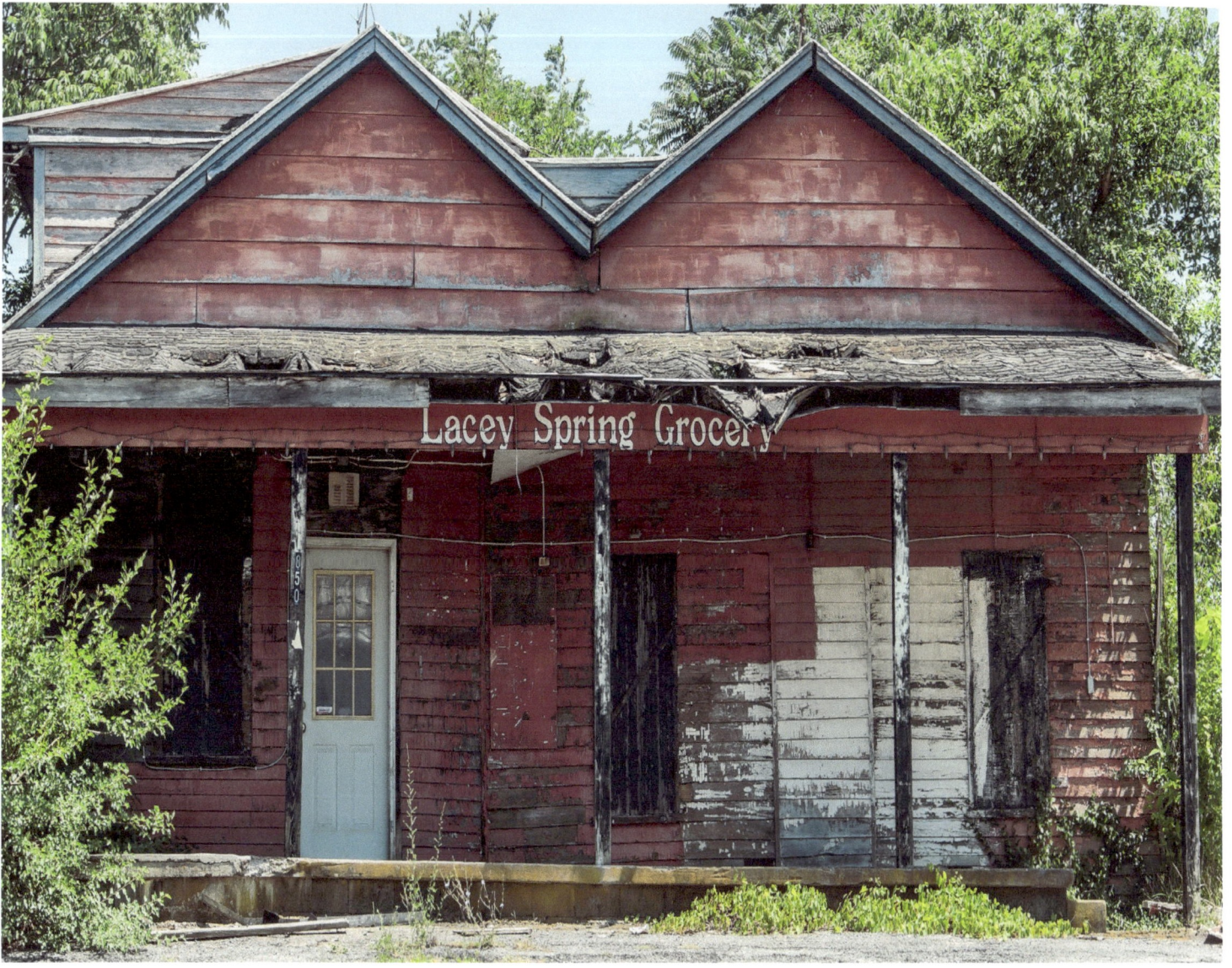

Lacey Spring Grocery, Lacey Spring, VA

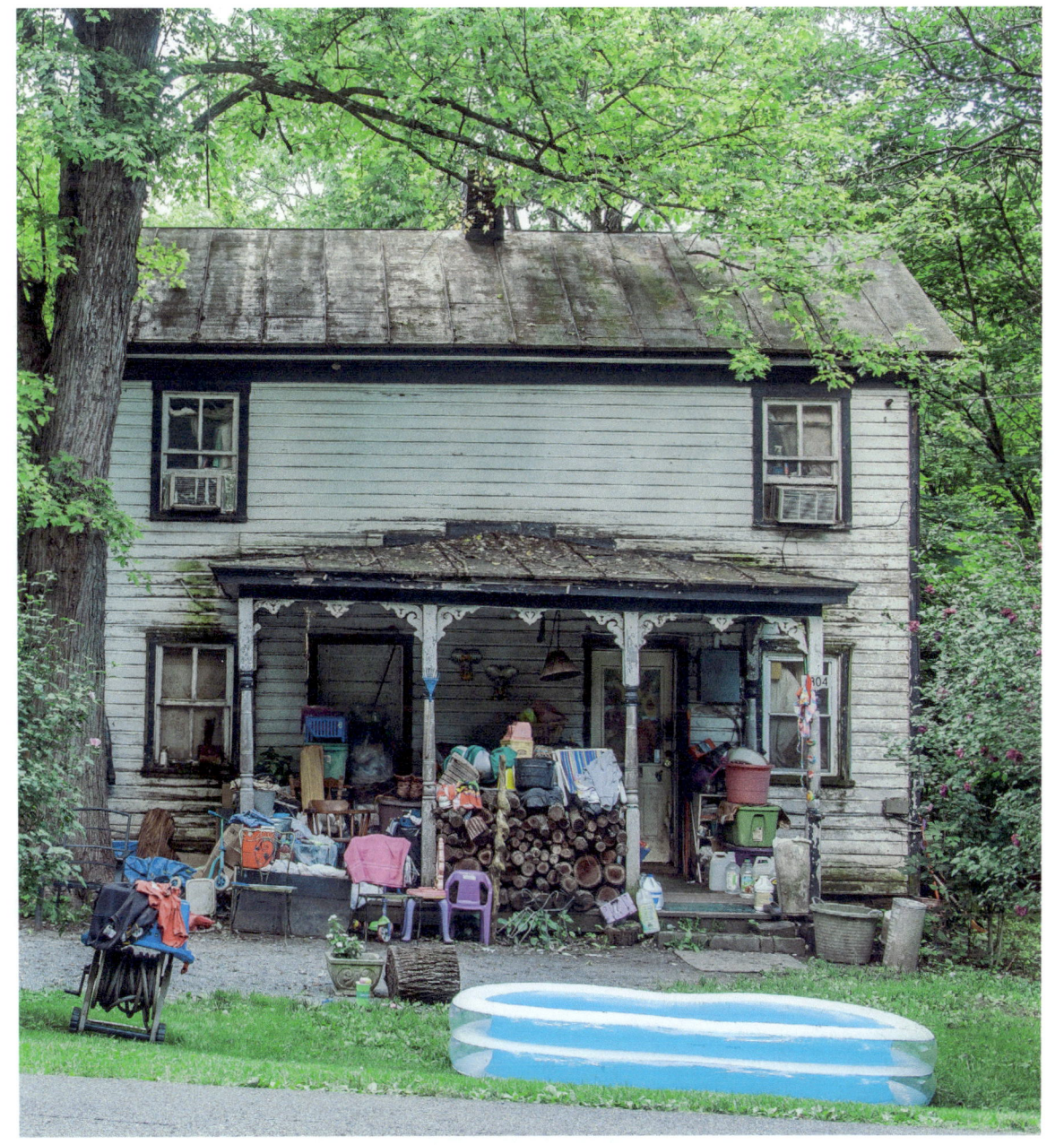

All Purpose Home, Millwood, VA

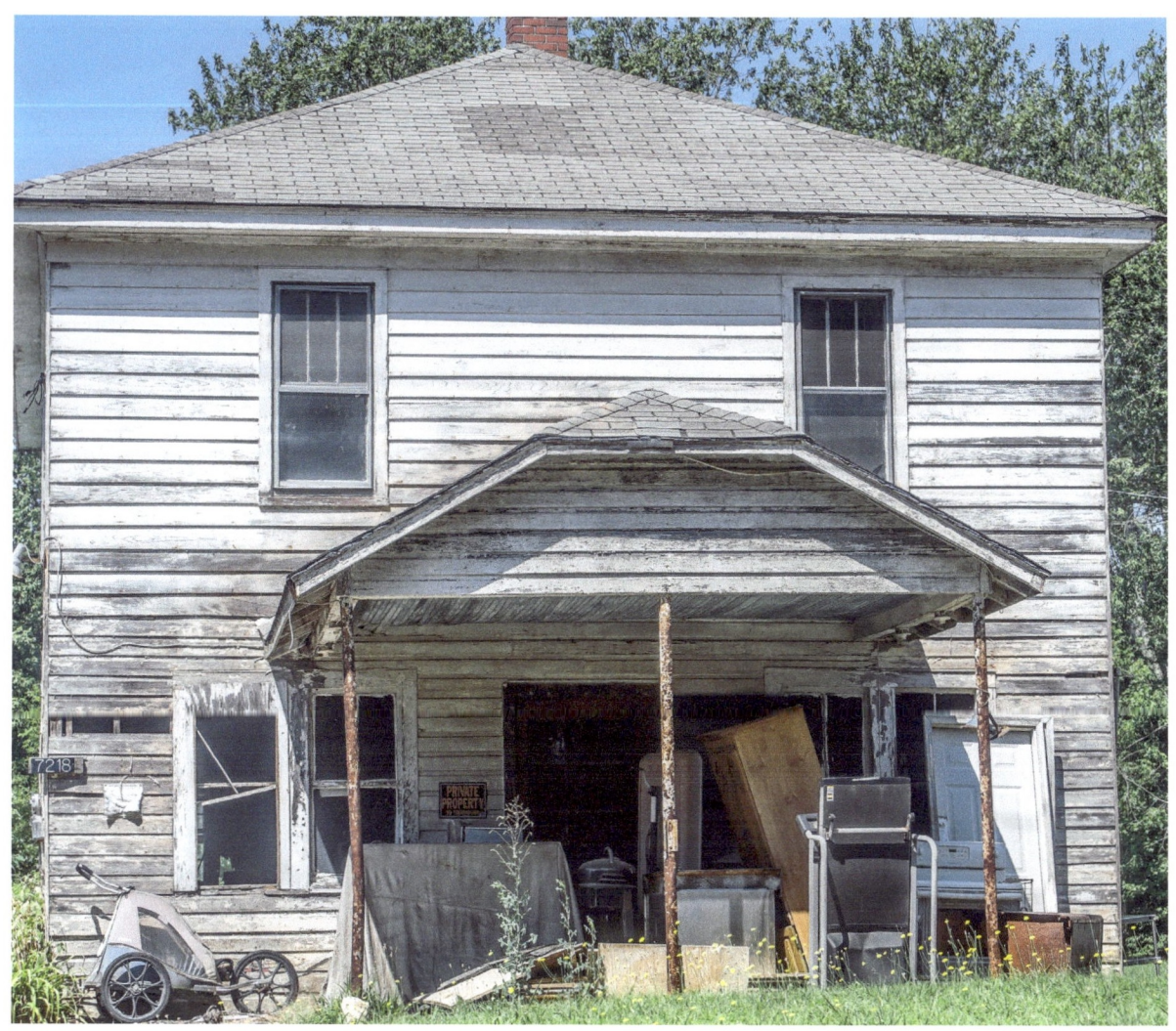

Old Repair Shop, Caroline County, VA

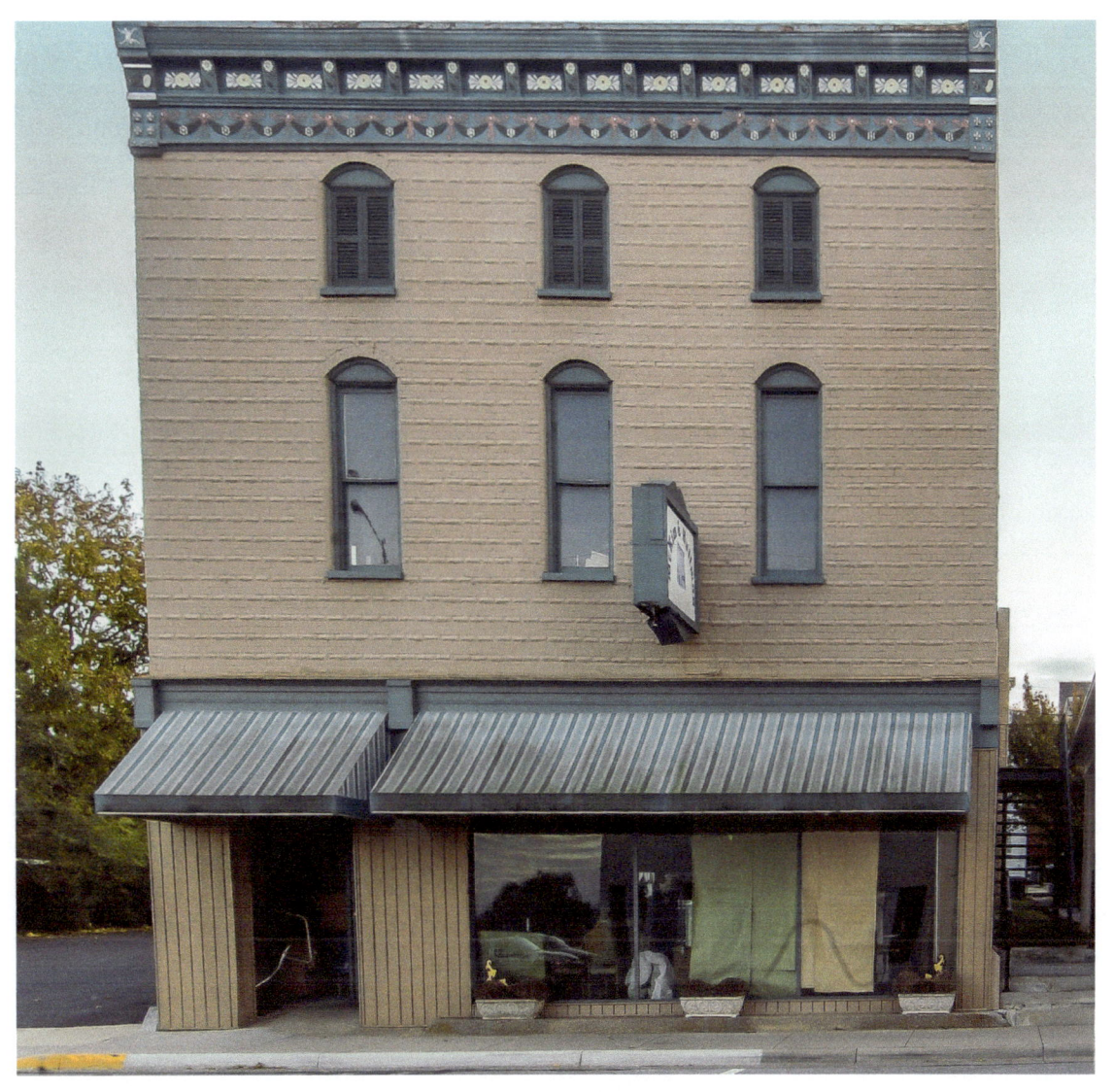

McKim & Huffman Drug Store, Luray, VA

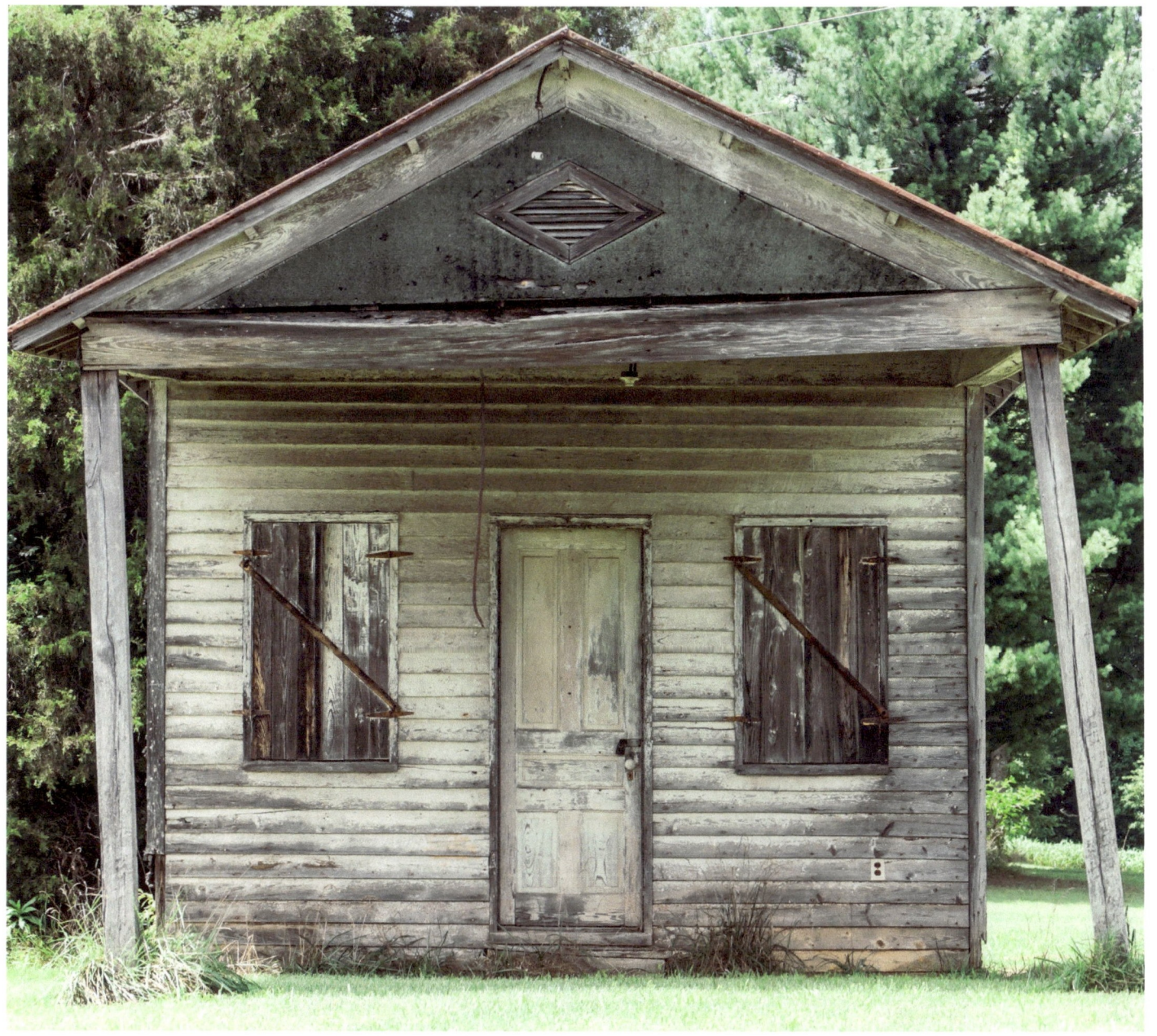

"This Old Home" - Locust Grove, VA

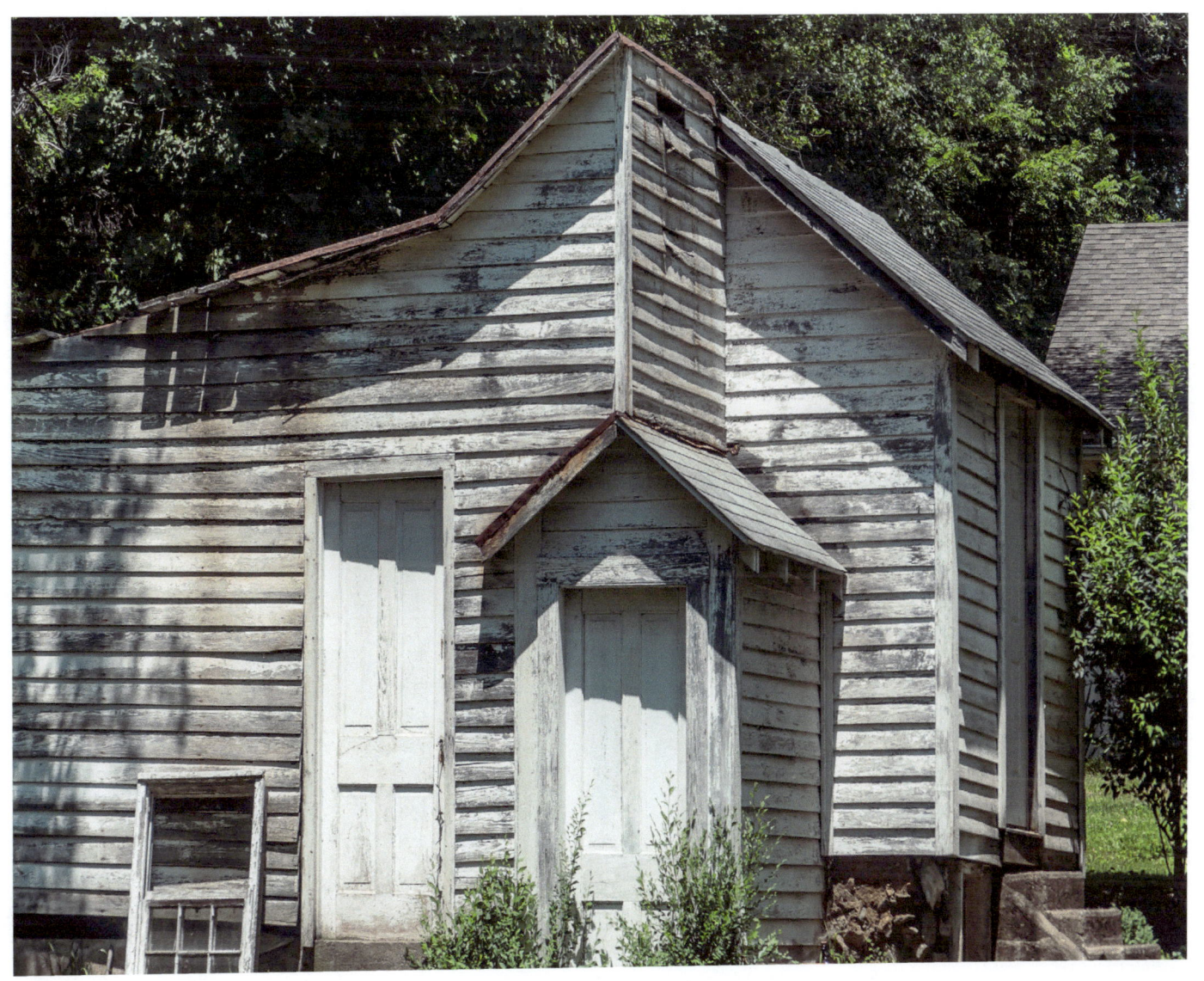

Unique Home, Upperville, VA

Doorless Porch, Port Royal, VA

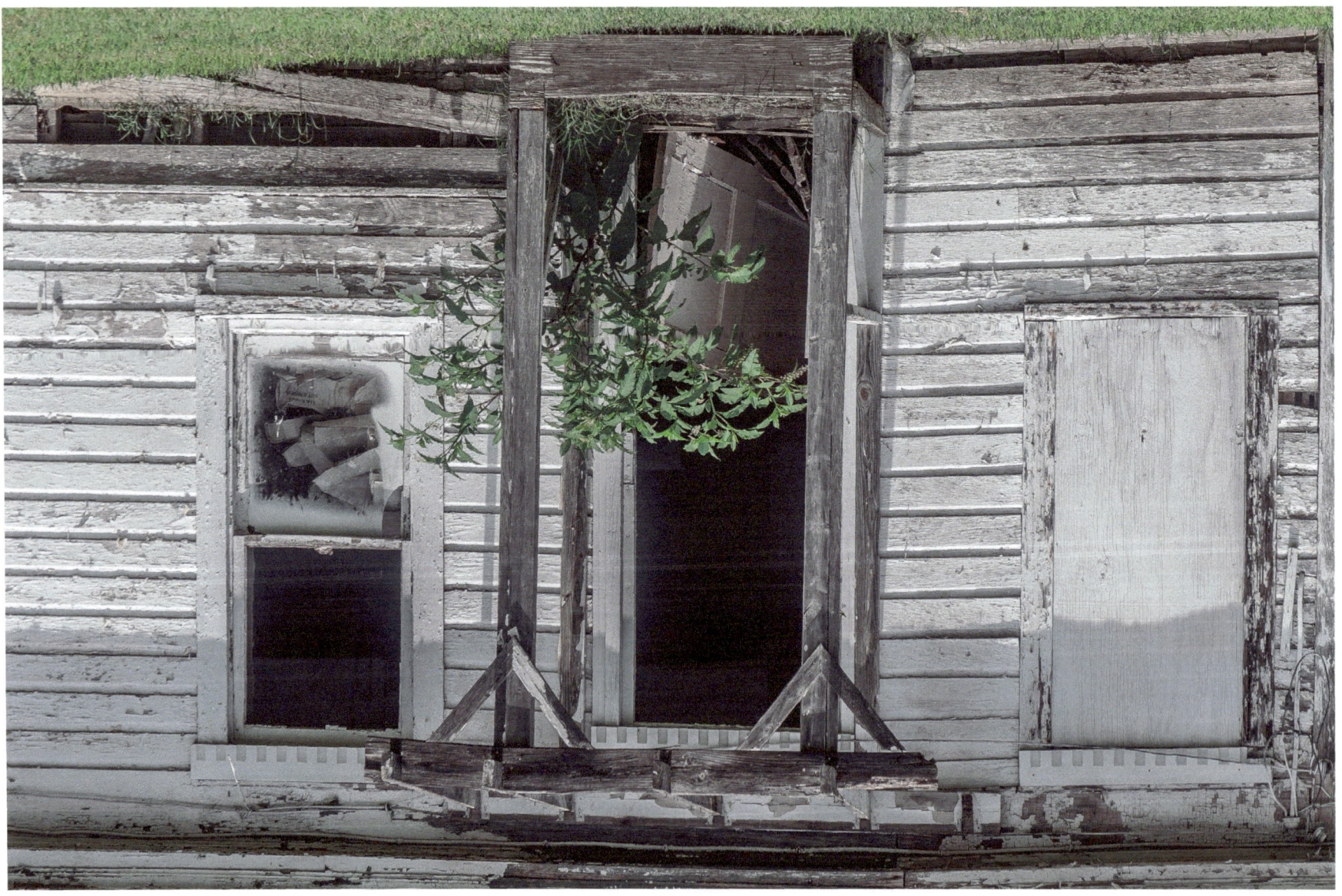

DECORATIVE FRONT PORCHES

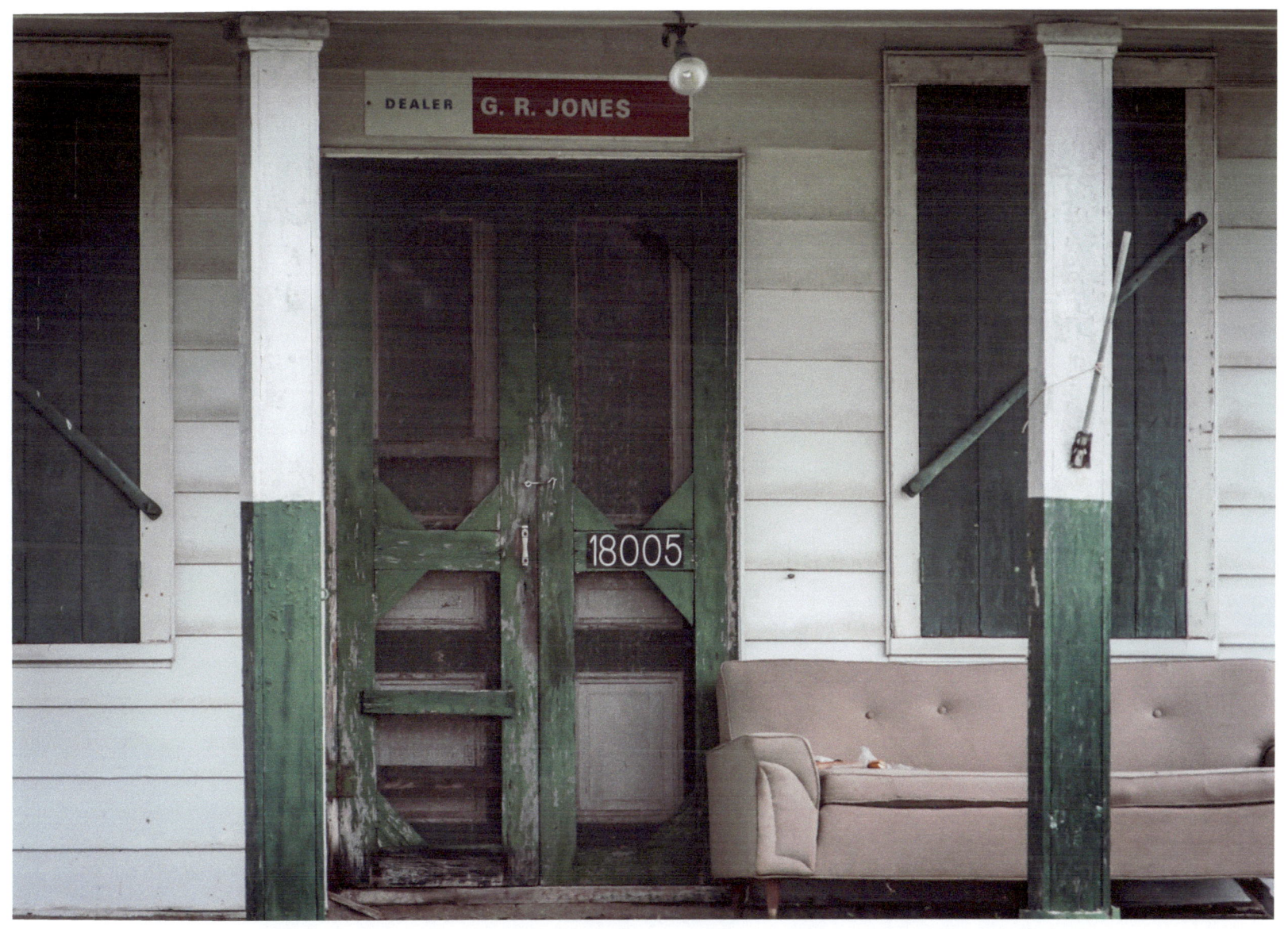

Dealer G. R. Jones, Unionville, VA

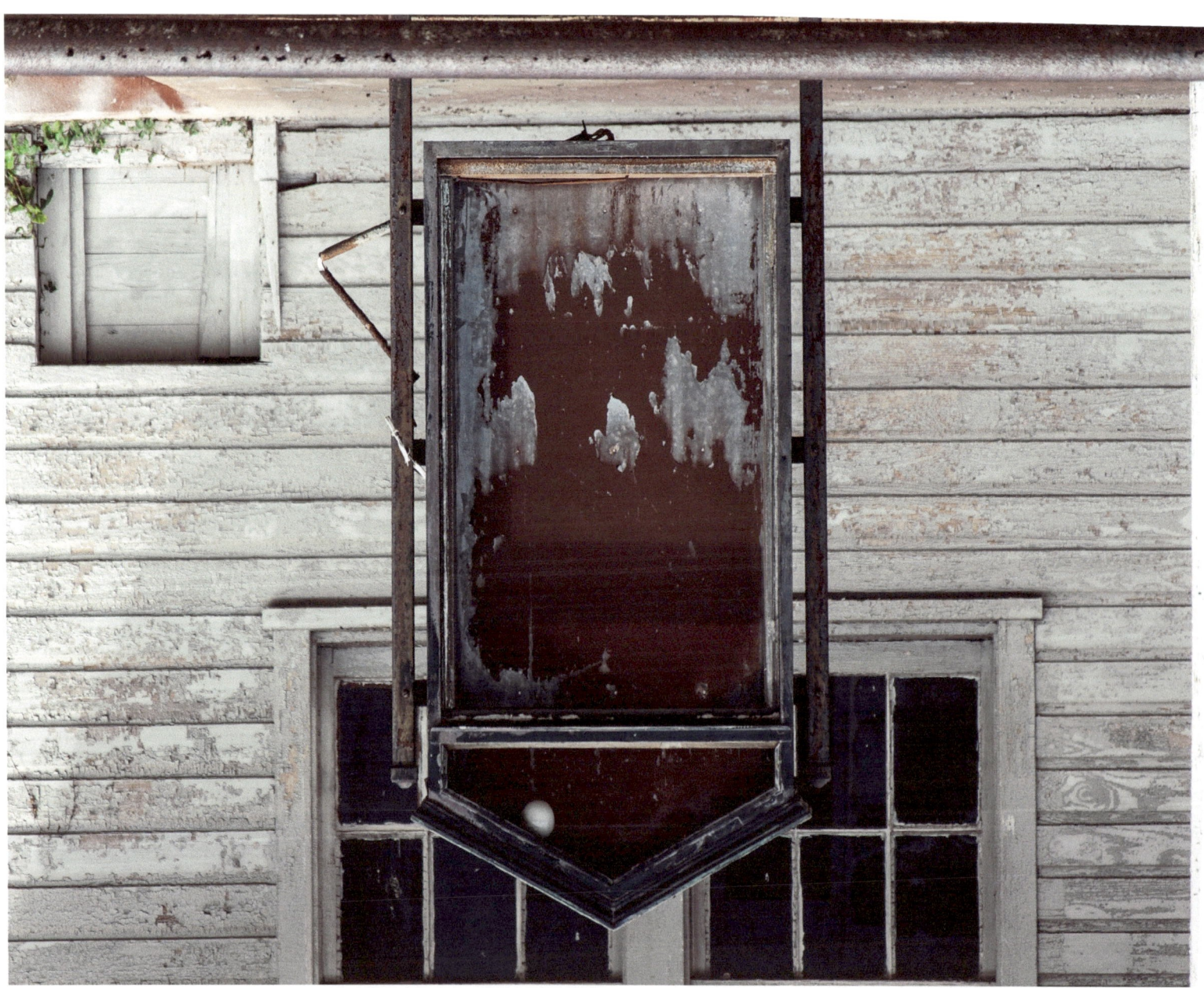

Andrew Jackson School, Luray, VA

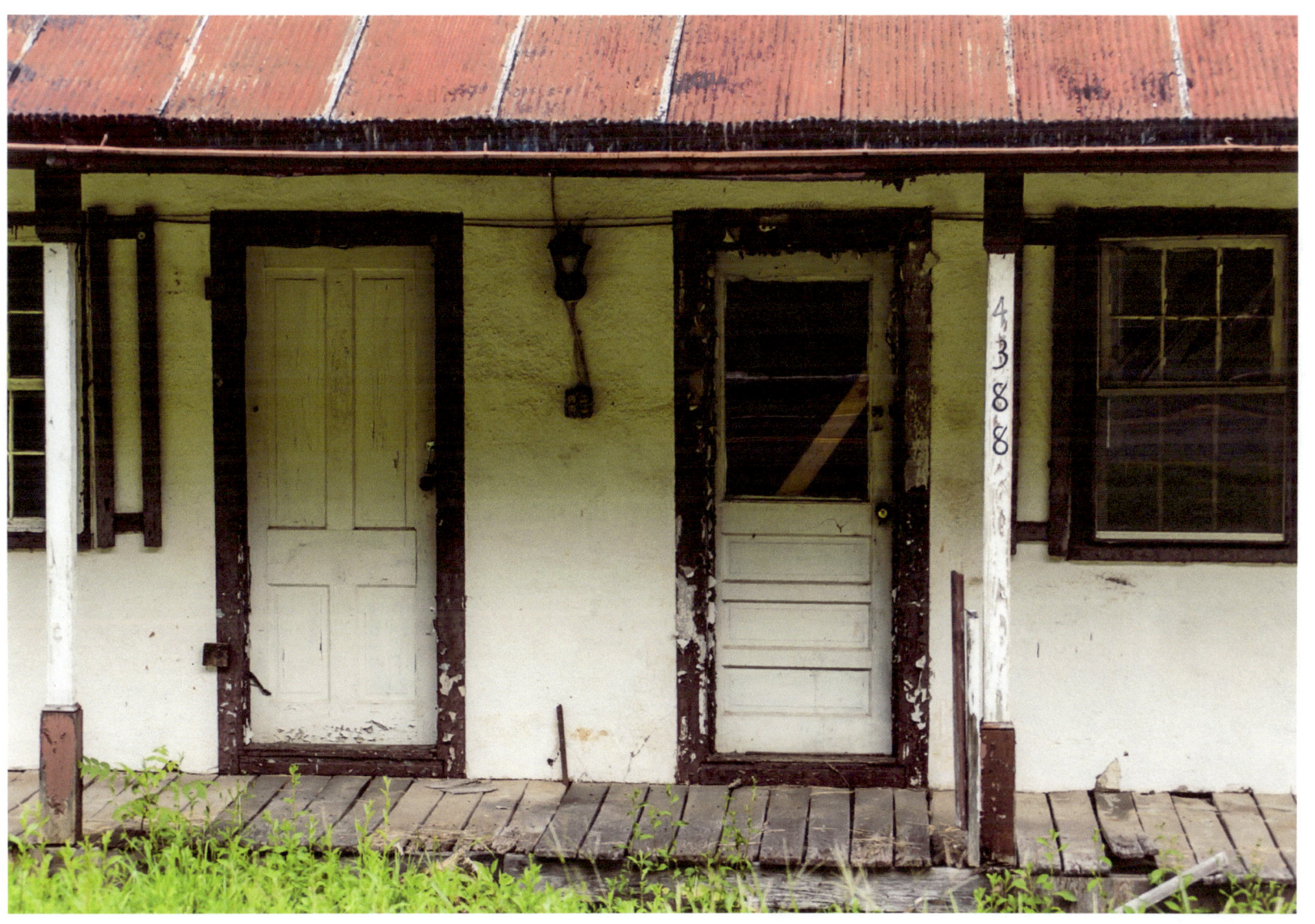

Colorful Wood Porch, The Plains, VA

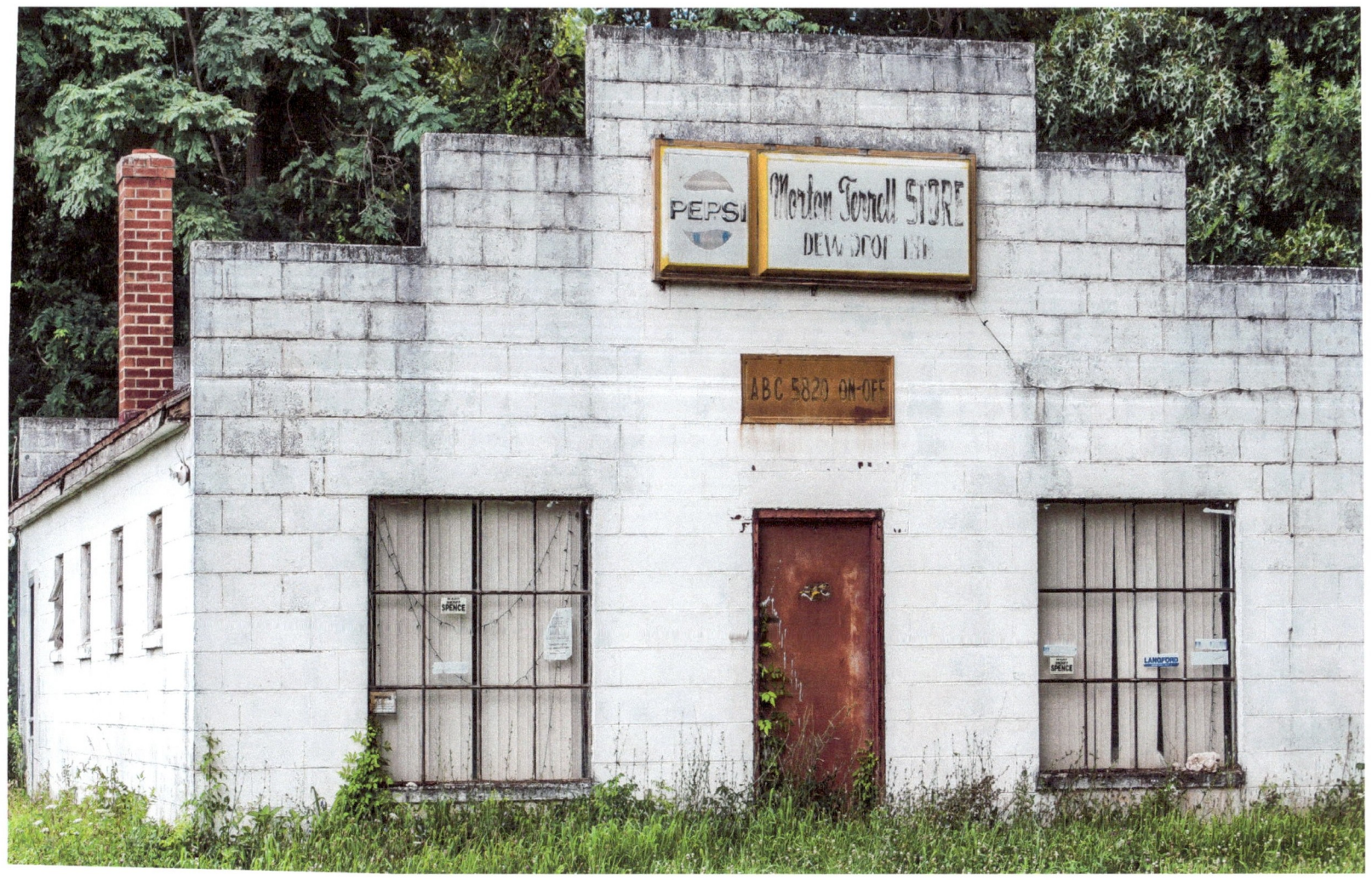

Morton Terrell's Dew Drop Inn, Unionville, VA

COMMUNITY CENTERS

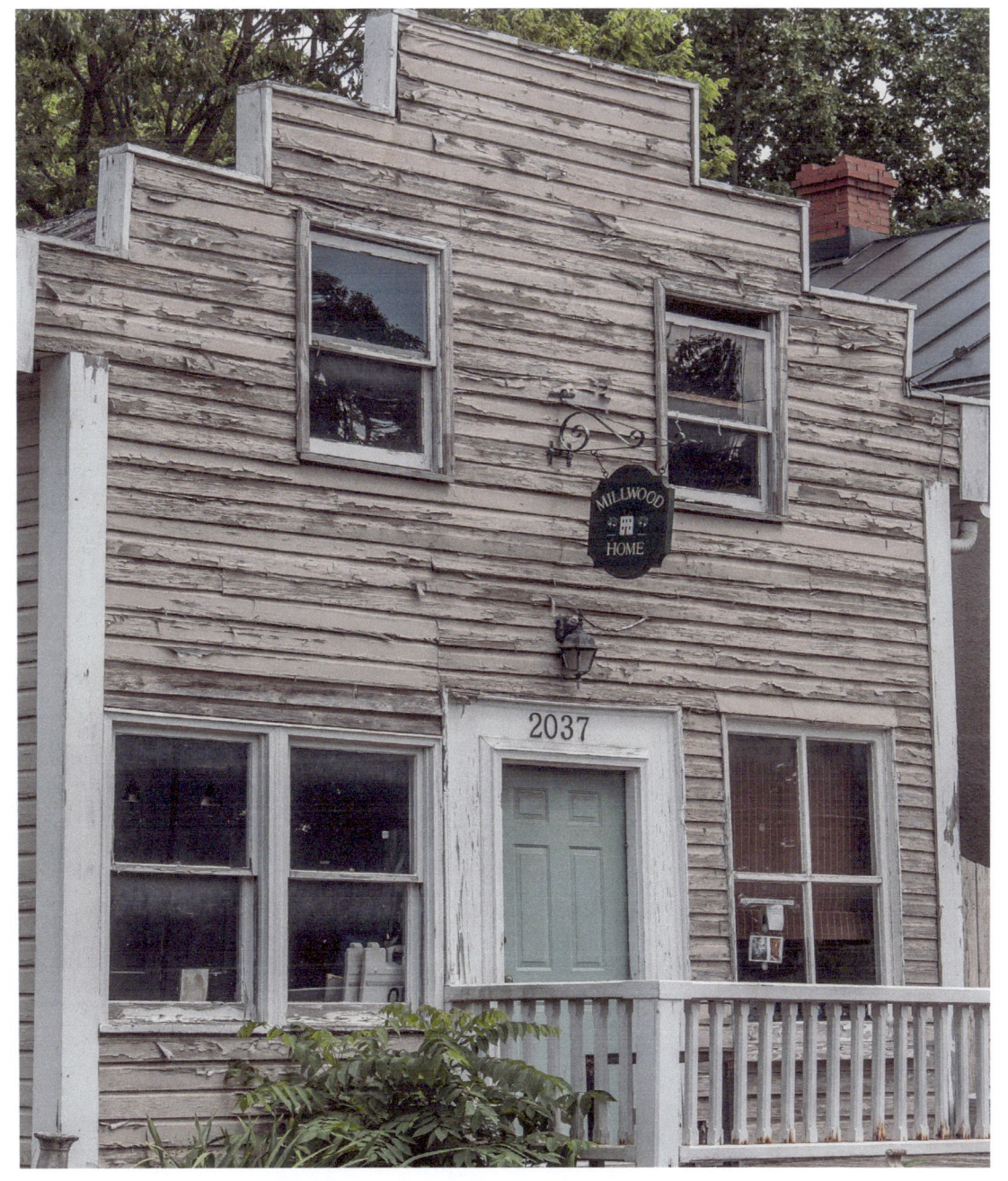

Millwood Home, Millwood, VA

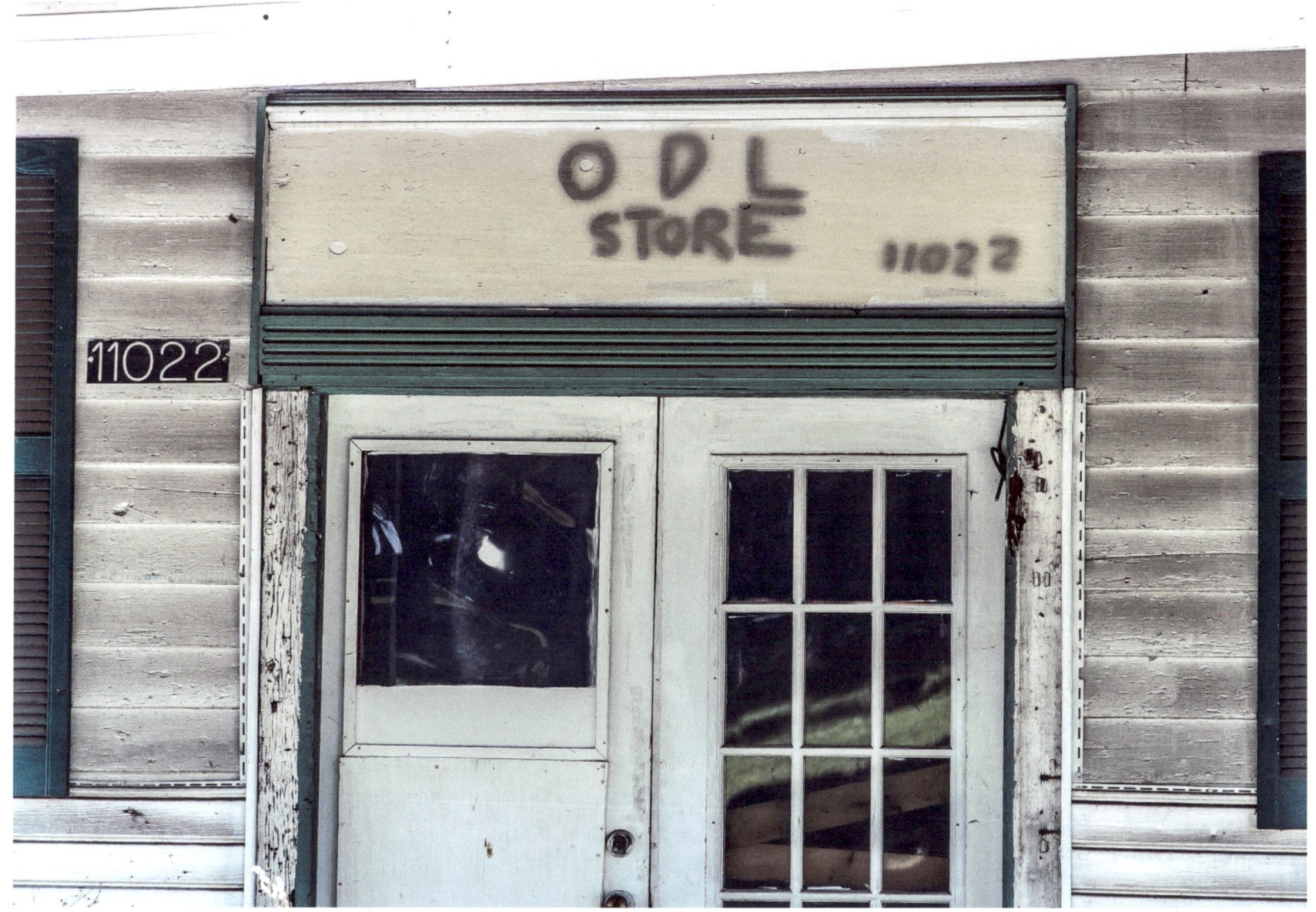

ODL Store, Mine Run, VA

OLD TIME GENERAL STORES

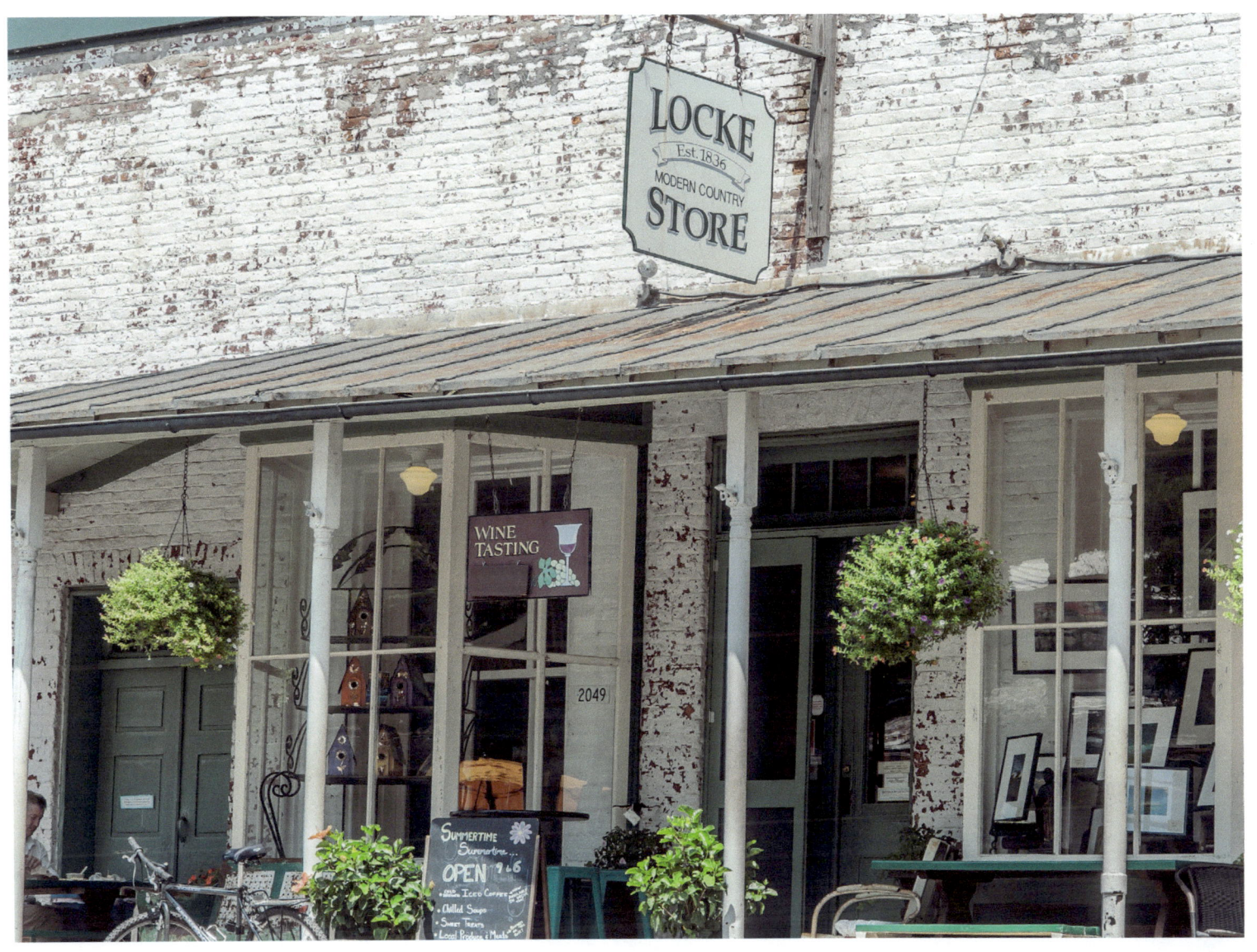

Locke Store, Millwood, VA

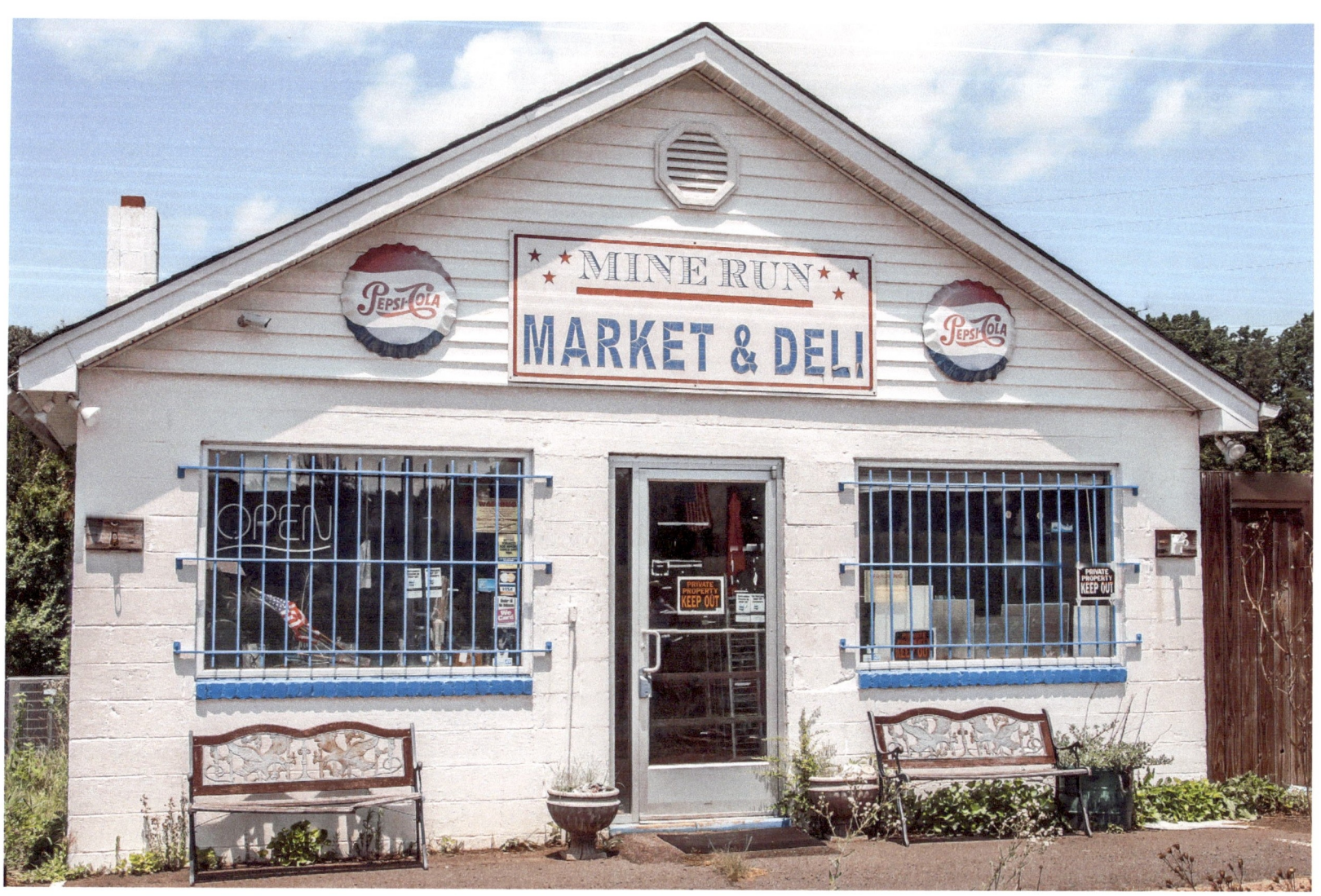

Mine Run Market & Deli, Mine Run, VA

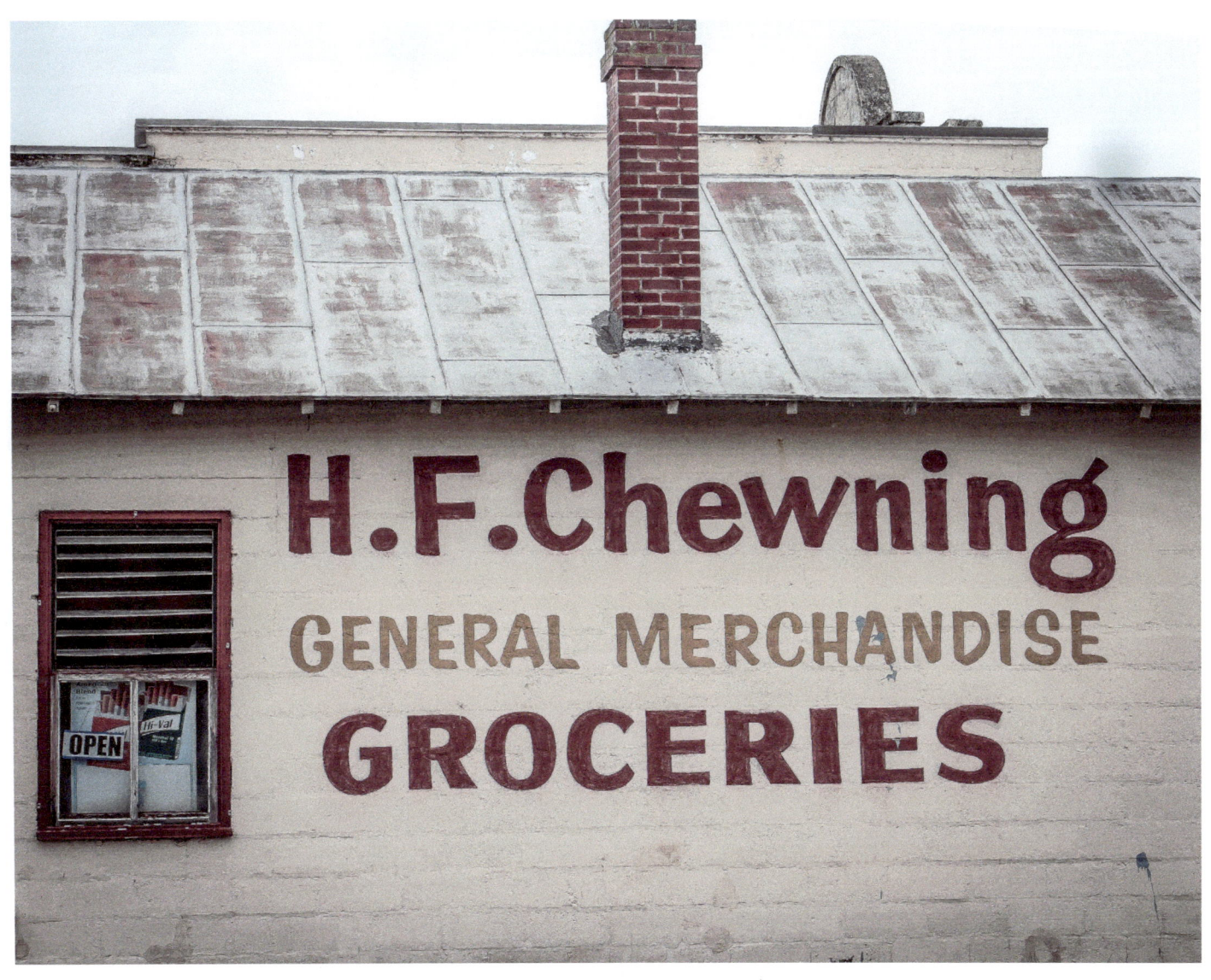

H. F. Chewning General Merchandise Groceries, Fredericksburg, VA

PRINTING PRESSES

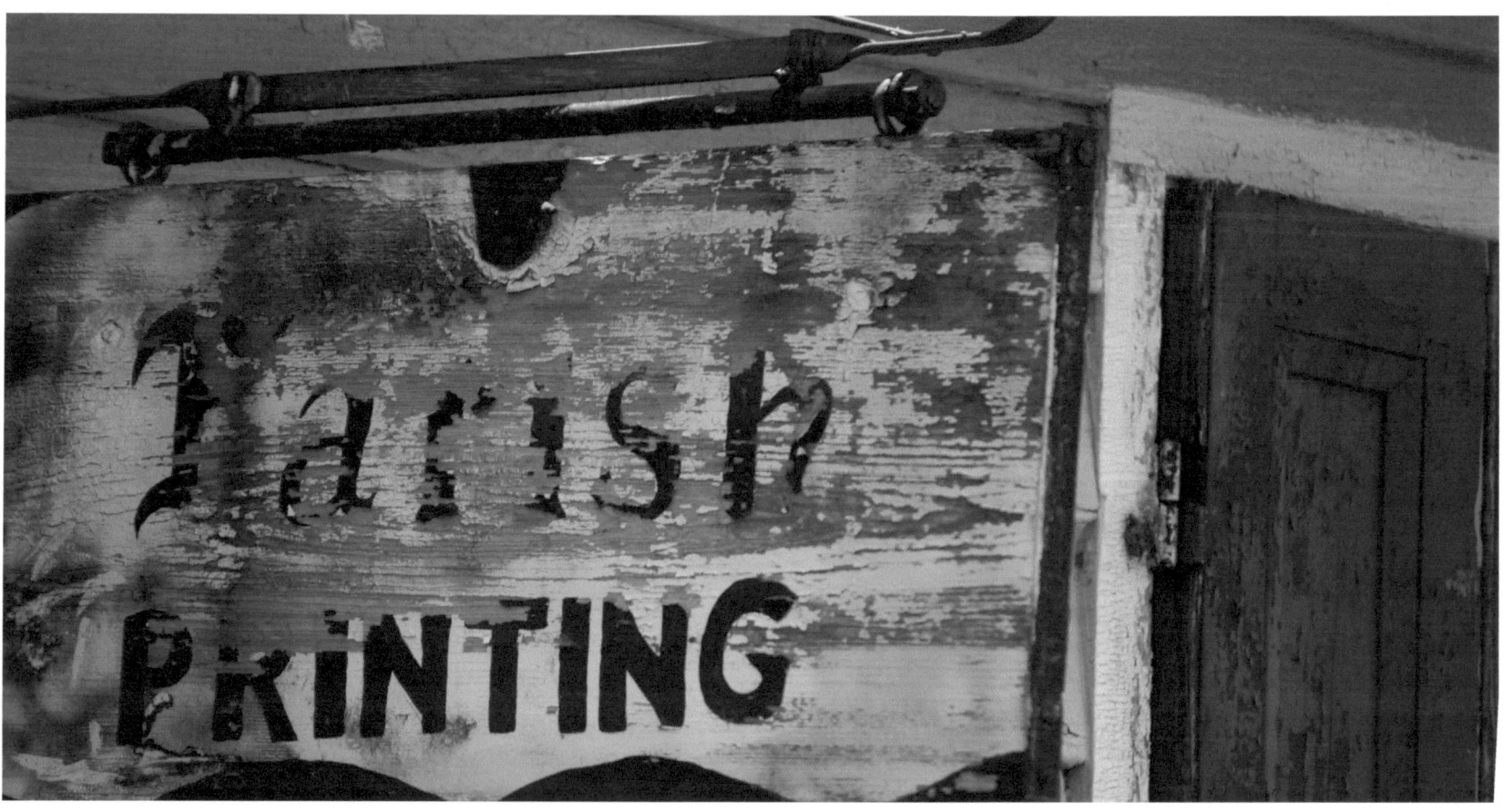

Parish Printing, Port Royal, VA

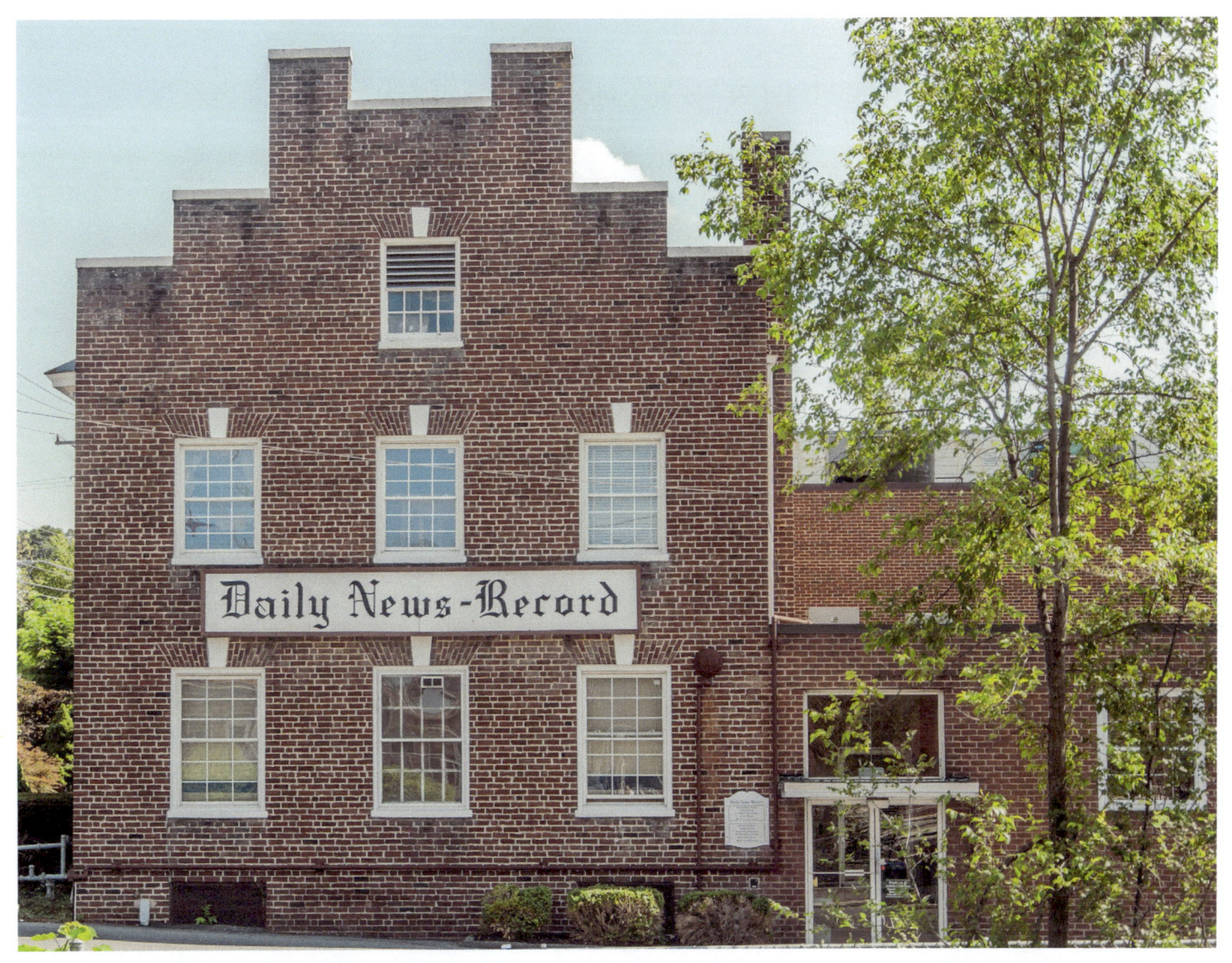

Daily News-Record, Harrisonburg, VA

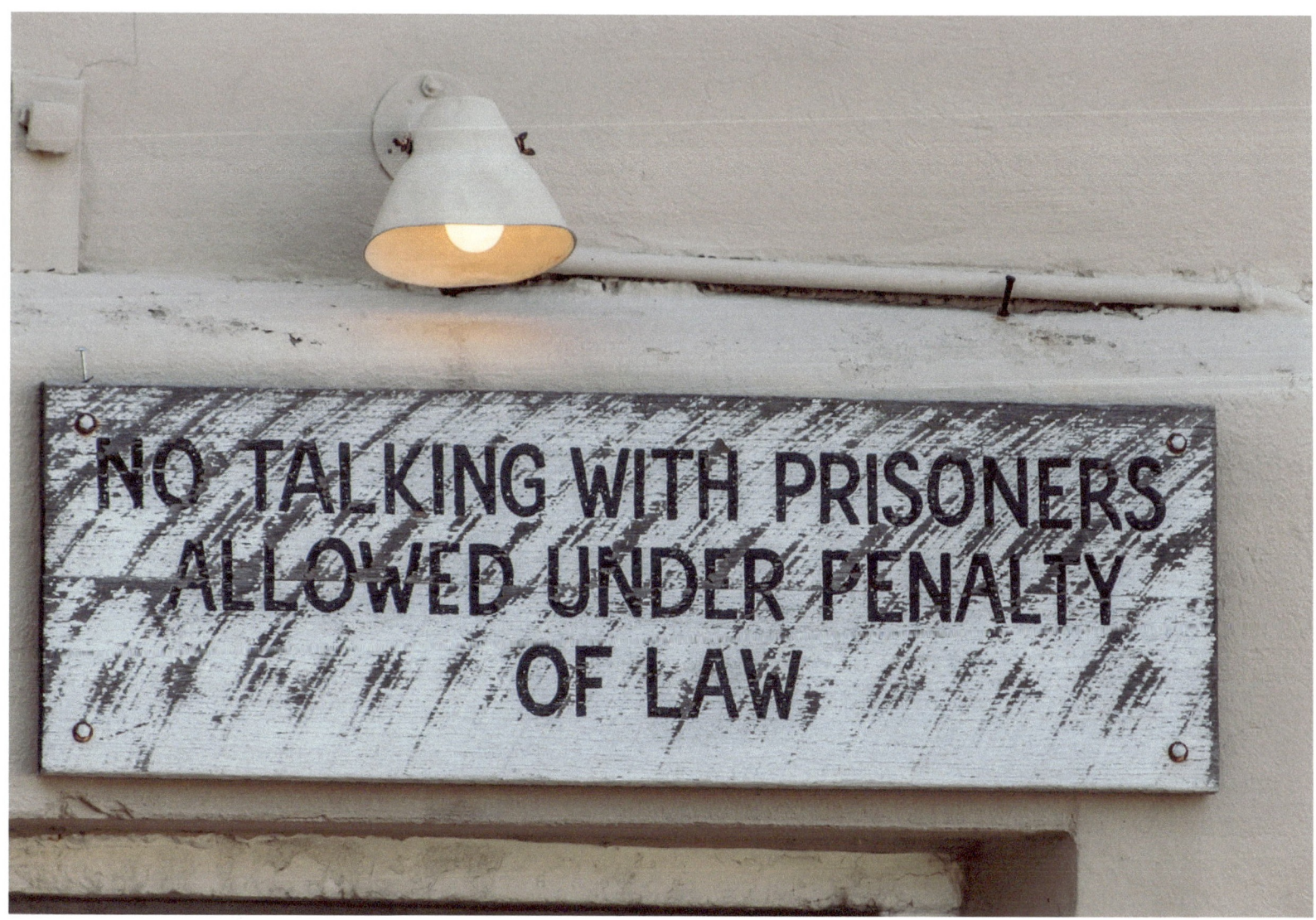

Sign at Fredericksburg's Old Jail, Fredericksburg, VA

UNIQUE SIGNS

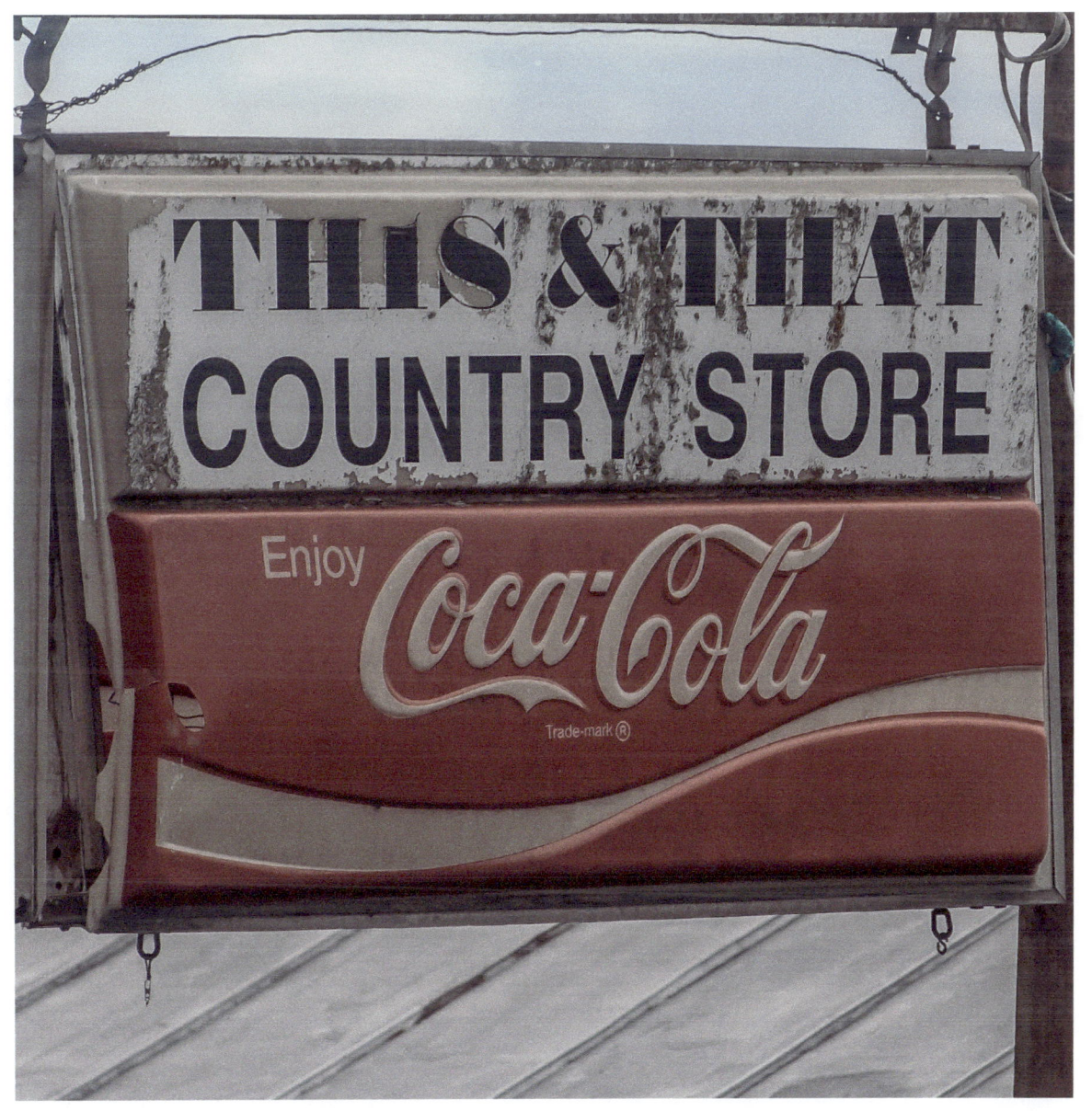

This & That Country Store, Quicksburg, VA

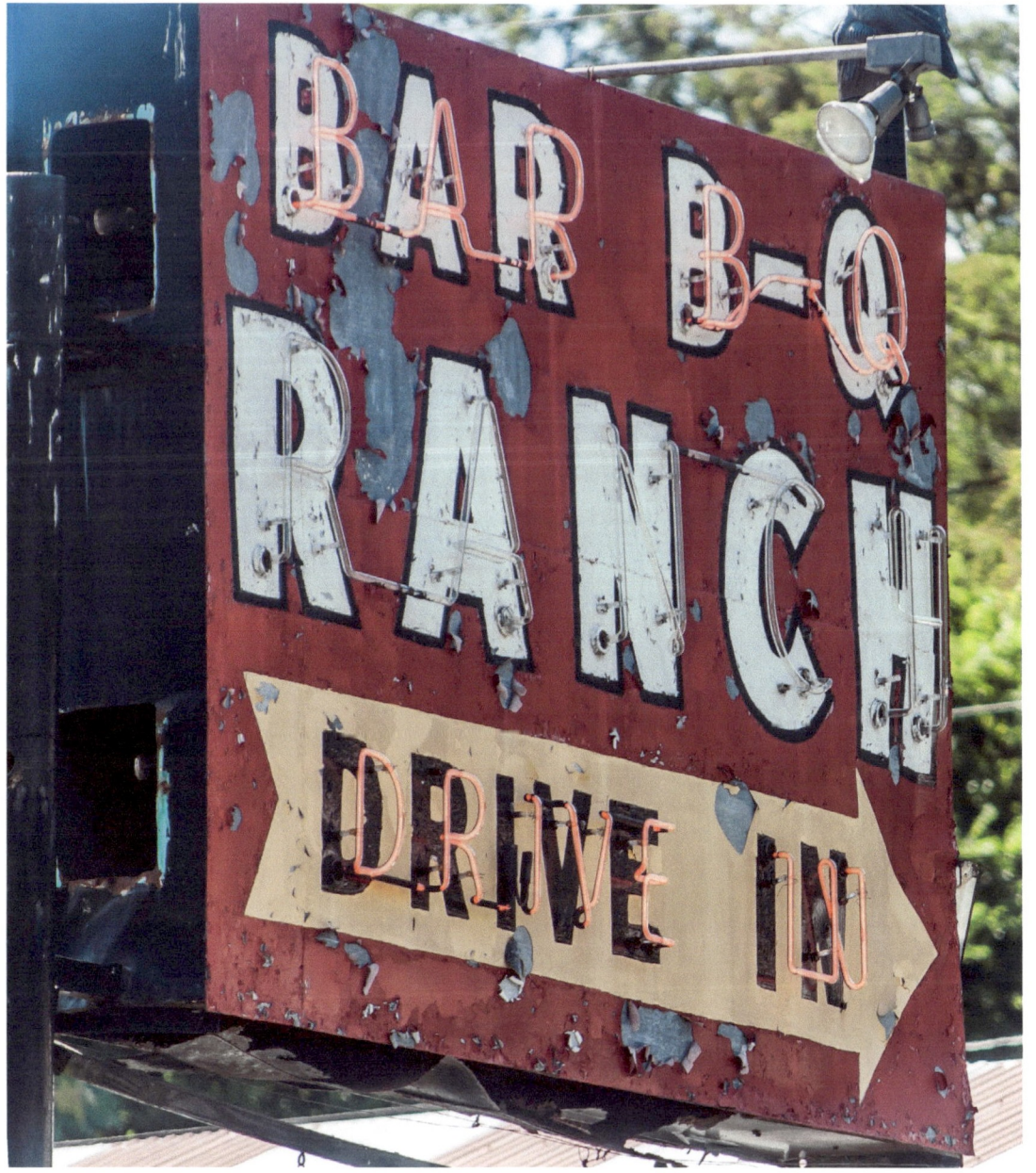

Bar B-Q Ranch Drive In, Harrisonburg, VA

SPECIALTY EATERIES

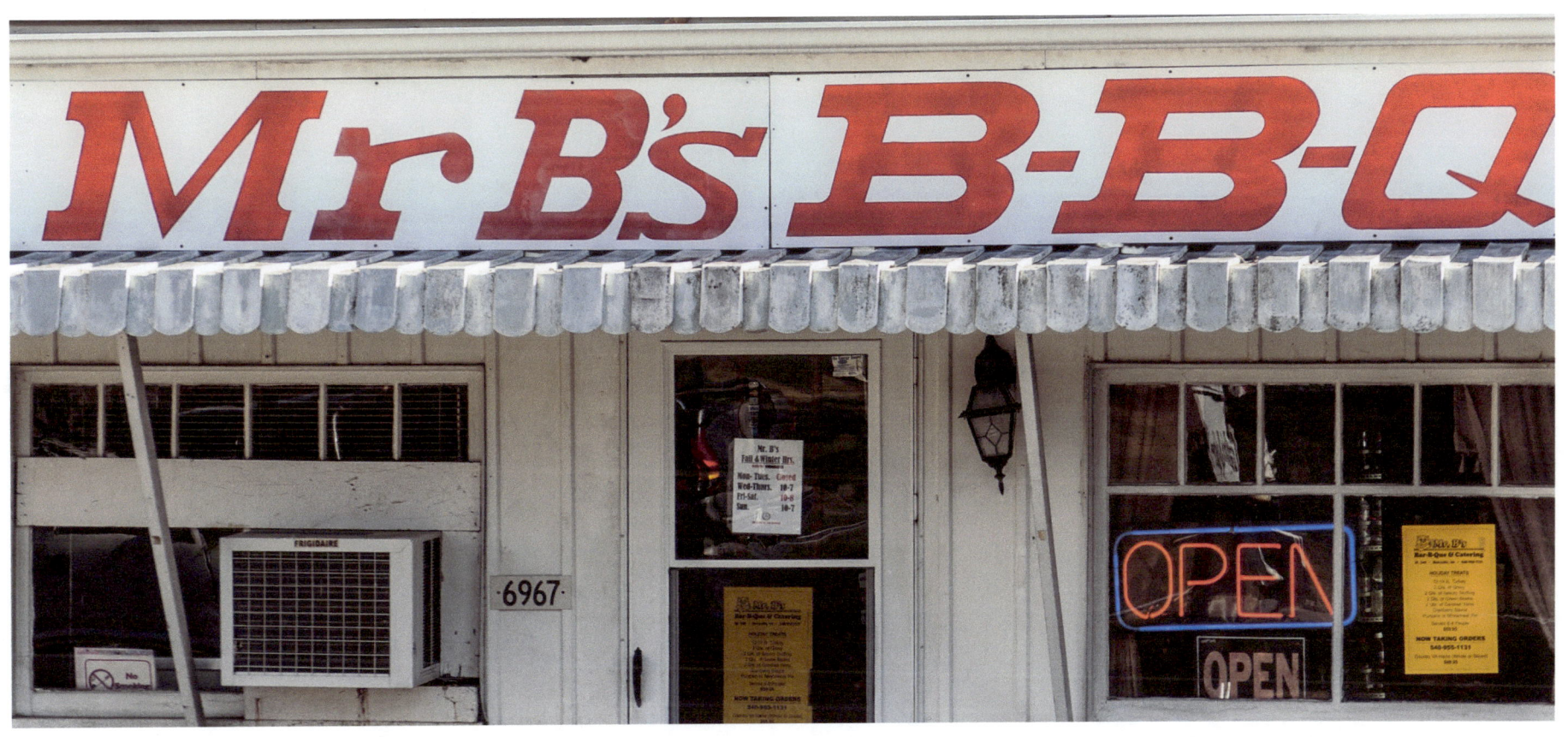

Mr. B's B-B-Q, Berryville, VA

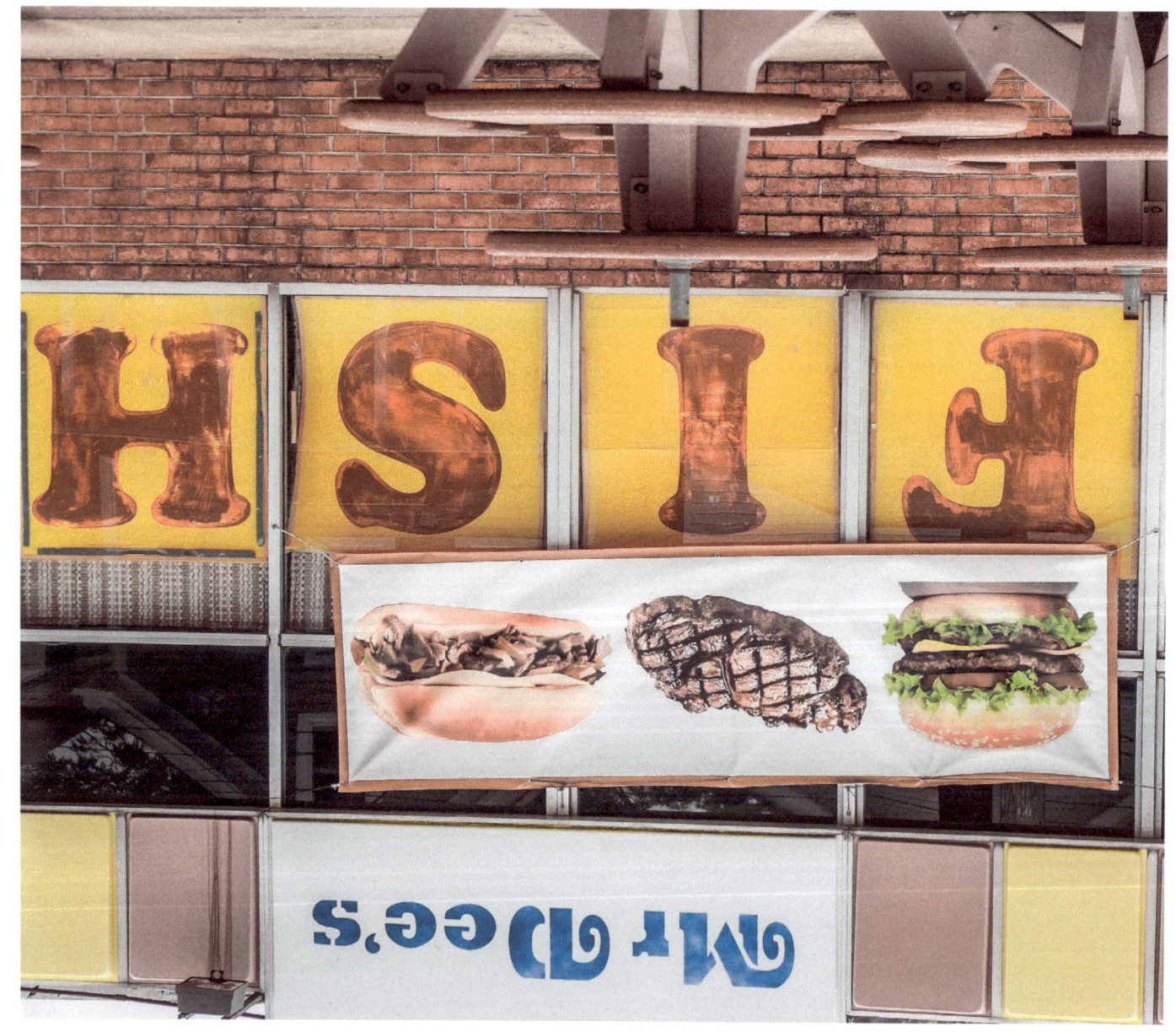

Mr. Dee's Fish, Fredericksburg, VA

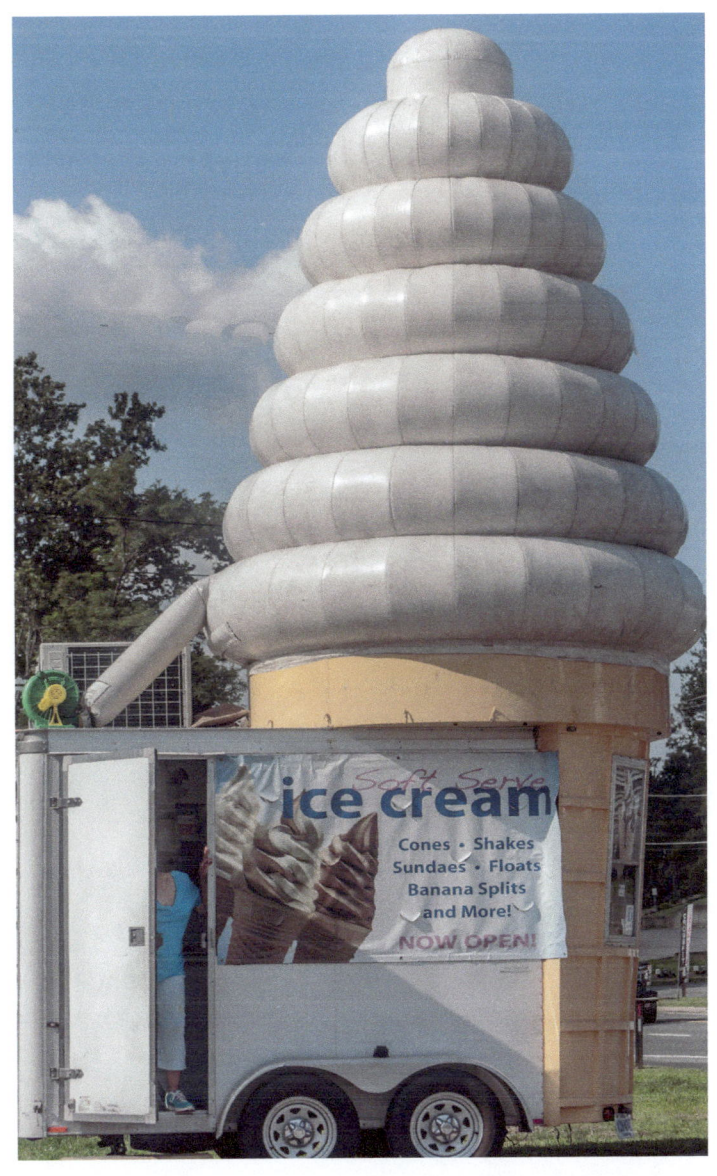

Soft Serve Trailer Stand, Stafford, VA

"HOME, SWEET HOME." - Harrisonburg, VA

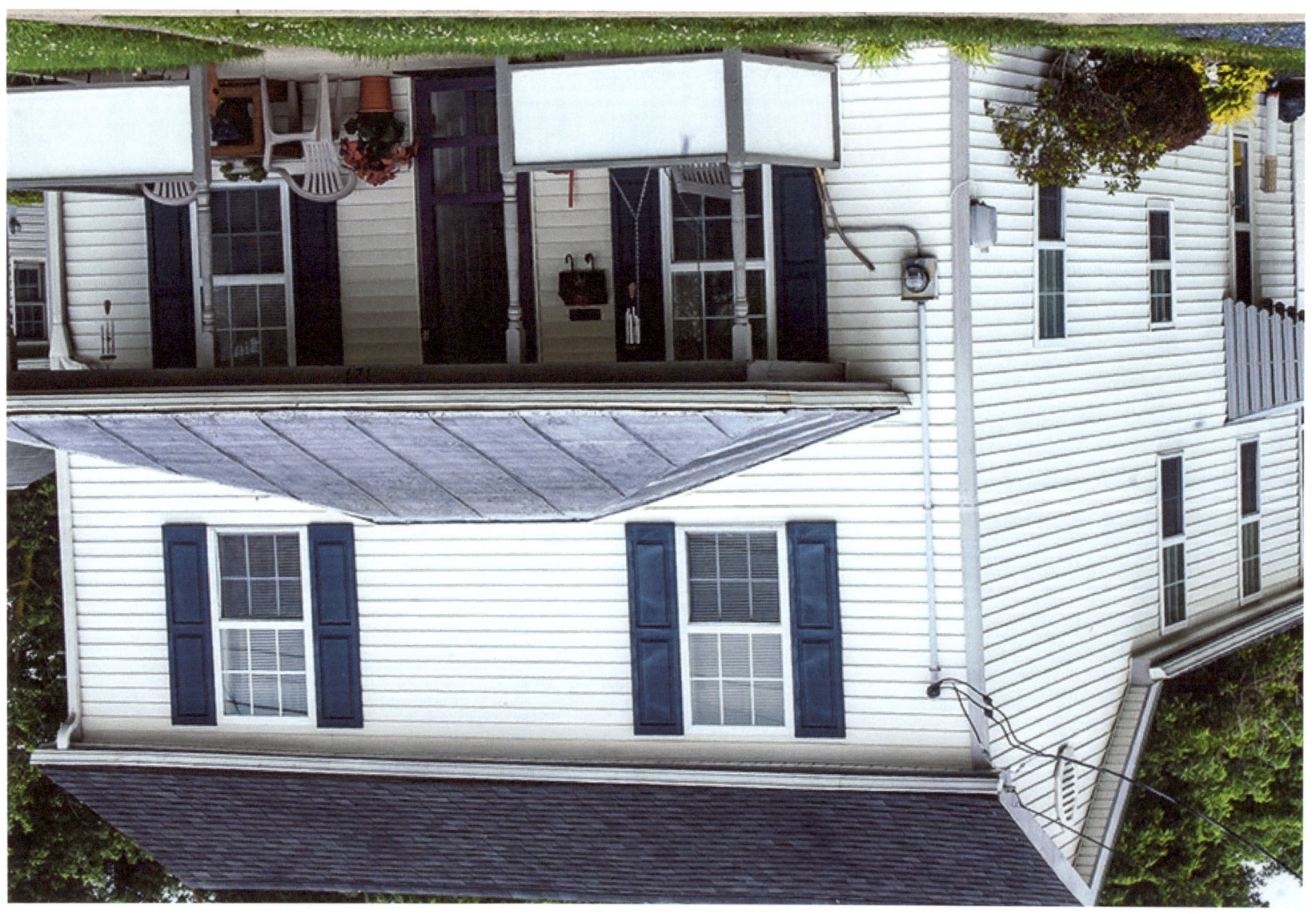

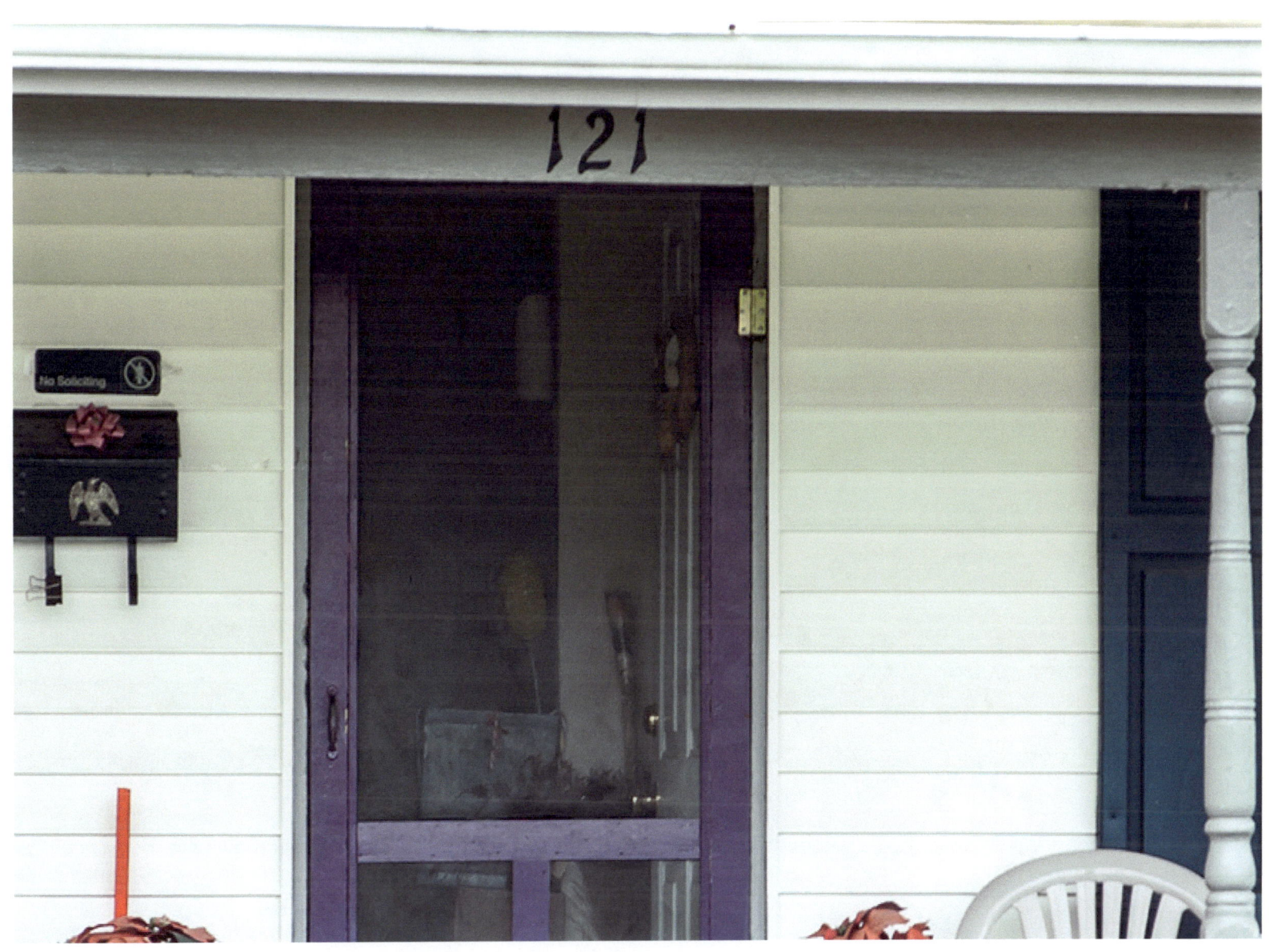

"WELCOME HOME"

Index

A
All Purpose Home 15
Antique Wagon Wheels and Vintage Bike 9

B
Bar B-Q Ranch Drive In 34
Berryville, VA 35
Bethel Baptist Church, est. 1890 2-3
Bowmantown, VA 1

C
Car Make
  1956 Dodge Pickup 13
  1956 Oldsmobile 12
Caroline County, VA 9
Colorful Wood Porch 23

D
Daily News-Record 31
Dealer G. R. Jones 21
Doorless Porch 20

F
Fredericksburg, VA 5
Furniture Store Door 6

G
Green Door Church 4

H
Harrisonburg, VA 31
H. F. Chewning General Merchandise Groceries, 29
Historic Building For Sale 5
"HOME, SWEET HOME" 38-39

L
Lacey Spring Grocery 14
Lacey Spring, VA 14
Locke Store, 27
Locust Grove, VA 18
Luray, VA 17

M
Macsville, VA 4
McKim & Huffman Drug Store 17
Milford, VA 6
Millwood Home, 25
Millwood, VA 8
Mine Run Market & Deli, 28
Mine Run, VA 26
Morton Terrell's Dew Drop Inn 24
Mr. B's B-B-Q, 35
Mr. Dee's Fish 36
Mt. Pleasant Baptist Church, est. 1875 1
Mural Bus 7

O
ODL Store 26
Old Repair Shop 16
Old School House 22

P
Parish Printing 30
Port Royal, VA 20

Q
Quicksburg, VA 33

R
Rusty VW Beetle 10

S
Sign at Fredericksburg's Old Jail, 32
Soft Serve Trailer Stand, 36
Stafford, VA 37
Spotsylvania, VA 12

T
The Plains, VA 23
"This Old Home" 18
This & That Country Store, 33

U
Unionville, VA 3
Unique Home 19
Upperville, VA 19

V
Vintage Chairs, 8
Vintage Trailer Bus 11